Recapitalism
For the Wealth
of People

Adam Gallagher

Copyright © 2023 Adam Gallagher
All rights reserved.

F.A.M.I.L.E.

Author's Note

Thank you for getting this far, and I hope you'll stick with it. I have sought to cram a fair bit into as few pages as possible. In doing so, I've tried to keep to the point, mostly avoiding autobiographical accounts, anecdotes, and self-serving stitch-together rehashes of other's people work, all of which frustrate me as a reader.

Essentially, two ideas are tabled in this book: firstly, a proposed focus shift in corporate ownership from profit to revenue – bottom line to topline. Secondly, a structured and remunerated crowd-based rating system that, in its application to capital markets, provides a benchmarking tool for investors. It also supports the pricing of finance for companies analogous to the service that major ratings agencies currently provide to a small fraction of the world's companies, though with a broad and decentralised approach.

The importance and supporting rationale for these ideas is set out in the context of reconciling human nature, welfare and prosperity with the economic system.

Thank you again for your interest and your time.

Contents

Introduction 1

PART I: A NEW HOPE 3

   1. Unleashing Human Potential: A New Dawn for Global Finance and Investment 5

   2. The New Era of Decentralised Economy: Work and Investment Unbounded 10

   3. Trust in Transition: Centralised to Decentralised 16

PART II: Cashflows, Shares, Obligation and Discontent: Tracing the Fault Lines of Capitalism 23

   4. Cashflows and Conflicts: The Dichotomy of Business Ownership 26

   5. Share ownership: The Concept, the Entitlement and the Conflict 31

   6. Steering Profit: The Intersection of Ownership, Control, and Operation 36

   7. Capitalism's Chameleons: The Shifting Landscape of Rules and Incentives 44

   8. Beyond Profit: The Morality of Business Purpose 49

PART III: The Currency of Existence: Time, Wealth, and Human Potential 61

   9. Perceiving the Worth of Human Wealth 63

   11. Towards Inclusive Capitalism:
Awakening the Entrepreneur Within 69

   11. Temporal Economics:
Unravelling the Human-Time-Money Trinity 75

**PART IV: THE NEED TO REIMAGINE INVESTMENT:
TOWARDS A MORE INCLUSIVE CAPITALISM 81**

12. Personification of Profits:
The Human and Corporate Dichotomy.............................. 83

13. Market Distortions
and the Inequity of Capital Raising..................................... 87

14. The Cost of Exclusion:
Capital Markets and the Democratisation of Investment .. 98

**PART V: : THE REVENUE REVOLUTION: DISRUPTING
TRADITIONAL INVESTMENT DYNAMICS 105**

15. Understanding where Investors sit in the
Conventional Cashflow Queue 109

16. A Paradigm Shift:
Reshaping the Agency-Owner Dynamics.......................... 123

17. Rebuilding Financial Markets: One Block at a Time ... 129

18. Revenue Tokens:
The Value Dawn of Decentralised Finance 135

19. Revenue Tokens:
The Confluence of Risk, Return, and Financing 140

**PART VI: RETHINKING REGULATION: THE COLLECTIVE
CONSCIENCE... 151**

20. Rewriting the Rules: Regulation Fit for the Future 155

21. From Reactive to Proactive:
Redefining the Regulatory Approach................................ 165

22. The Quest for a Fully Informed Market:
A Pursuit of Investor Equality 177

PART VII: A NEW ERA FOR INVESTMENT RATINGS AND THE COST AND AVAILABILITY OF CAPITAL......... 183

    23. Harnessing the Wisdom of the Crowd:
A New Era for Investment Ratings and the Cost
and Availability of Capital 187

    24. In Pursuit of Democratic Capitalism:
The Universal Crowd Rating... 195

    25. Calculating and Applying
the Universal Crowd Rating 203

    26. Rating Contributor Incentives and Compensation..... 215

PART VIII: THE RISE OF DECENTRALISED CAPITAL MARKETS: COEXISTENCE, EVOLUTION AND LATERAL DISRUPTION 225

    27. Three Pillars of Novel Financial Instruments:
Issuers, Investors and Marketplace 229

    28. The UCR:
Bridging Profit and Revenue-Centric Paradigms.............. 236

    29. Accountability in the Decentralised Realm:
Mastering Destiny.. 243

    30. Redefining Capitalism: A 'Human-centric' Approach. 247

    Recapitalism:
The Manifestation of a New Capitalist Paradigm............. 252

    About the Author 259

    References 260

INTRODUCTION

The judicious application of emerging technologies often disrupts certain conventions—for the better. A contemporary version of this is the potential demo-cratisation of capital markets. A true democratic ethos is poised to emerge, grounded not in the often muddled and distorted manifestations of Western politics, but in the more direct spirit of 'power to the people'. This heralds a shift towards a world where the legacy barriers between individuals and their wealth, creativity, and self-worth are dismantled, ultimately aligning society more closely with its innate human nature.

Human beings were not designed to be mere interchangeable components in a vast machine; each person is uniquely endowed with a distinct brilliance that ought to be expressed. Time and resources are finite, and for the collective good of society, the communal structures, processes and outcomes that dictate modern life should prioritise the maximisation of each individual's potential.

Renowned twentieth-century philosopher of science, Thomas Kuhn, highlighted the pervasive, deeply ingrained paradigms within which individuals operate.[1] These paradigms often seem so fitting and logical during their reign that the very thought of questioning them rarely occurs to most, and the protective din of the status quo quickly silences those that do.

However, history has demonstrated that paradigms, regardless of their perceived invincibility, have always proven transient, and are displaced by new paradigms. When this occurs, the sacred principles of the obsolete paradigm collapse and the adherents of the new one find it hard to believe that their predecessors could ever have subscribed to such a notion. The power of incumbency provides robust protection for a paradigm as nature abhors a vacuum, and the prevailing paradigm, no matter how beleaguered or moribund, will never spontaneously implode. The incumbent paradigm is anchored by its vast array of beneficiaries, and any alternative must offer overwhelming superiority to effect change. Conversion starts with humility and loss, which most people are inclined to avoid or delay.

If the quickest way to stress test an interpersonal relationship is to introduce money, how great, then, is the challenge of contending with billions of people from diverse places, cultures, religions and languages to develop sustainable systems of transacting, where the common good and the individual good are sufficiently aligned to genuinely afford each person the best opportunity of celebrating what it means to be human; To enjoy and deploy their unique energies, emotions, and creativity.

Capitalism has been instrumental in lifting billions from poverty, spurring significant innovation and infusing the human experience with deep-seated meaning across many arenas. However, the extent of its collateral damage —as practiced—to global human and environmental wealth, health and welfare is of increasing concern.

However, at some point, spirited conversations must give way to action as change hinges on the 'how', not the 'why'. Historical evidence consistently attests that any initiative aiming at societal transformation, regardless of how beneficent its proponents purport it to be, must necessarily begin with economic restructuring. Otherwise, it has no foundation in human nature and will likely fail with a systemic misread of the subject matter.

While the extent of 'equality of success' may be contingent on an individual's endeavours and fortune, the manifestation of 'equality of opportunity' is inherent to the system's structure. Emerging technologies present novel prospects to enhance this noble global social and economic goal. The advent of technological breakthroughs should consequentially inspire a re-evaluation of the prevailing foundational principles. Absent this reflective interlude, new technologies merely accelerate old practices, whereas their true potential lies in facilitating systemic structural transformations.

The profit-motive, a cornerstone of capitalism, owing to the conventional approach to corporate ownership structure, compels companies to strive to maximise net cashflows. The pragmatic role of the profit-motive resides in its ability to sustain companies and generate returns for their owners. However, profit in the context of capitalism has ascended to a position of supreme importance, relegating all other considerations and reducing more holistic human values that transcend the simple arithmetic of debits and credits.

'Freedom' is the rallying cry of capitalism, but for many, the profit motive does not evoke a sense of liberty but implies obligation, which may not align with their inclination. The global expansion in the number and scale of enterprises existing under the precept of the profit-motive has exacerbated a fragmentation of human focus, resulting in an increasing compartmentalisation of compassion as stakeholders lose sight of the humanity of their counterparts within the system.

Seventeenth-century philosopher, Blaise Pascal, posited that individuals only take a step forward in pursuit of their happiness.[2] Incentives towards perceived satisfaction thus direct their path. A misalignment of these incentives muddies the water and impedes each individual's journey. For virtue to hold more than a fleeting circumstantial significance, it necessitates a structural paradigm that lays the groundwork for shaping these incentives.

The absence of empathy and alignment generates friction, which detracts from productivity and quality of life. 'Structural alignment' is instrumental in fostering peace amongst transacting individuals who lack personal bonds or mutual care. When one stakeholder's perceived good aligns with another's, they naturally pursue the same goal, irrespective of their sentiments towards each other. Conversely, discord ensues when one individual's aspirations infringe upon another's interests.

Modern discourse on social and environmental issues appears incongruous with the profit-motive. The profit-motive cannot sensibly fit into the context of emerging social philosophies when companies are created for the one-overriding purpose: delivering financial returns to their owners, which, with the profit-centric ownership model, implies an obligation to maximise profit.

This pervading obligation is increasingly being called out as the enemy of contemporary societal concerns, and the baby risks being thrown out with the bath water with growing calls to resurrect the redundant ideological traps of social engineering. A simpler notional question could be posited without wholesale economic destruction:

Is profit-based corporate ownership the best systemic reconciliation with humanity?

And more so,

Is it possible for companies to strive to enrich all stakeholders in the broadest sense?

Idealism stands no chance on the playing field against obligation and incentive, and without systemically addressing those two formative behavioural elements, there will be no lasting shift.

While money is an essential tool for most individuals, entrepreneurs are typically driven first and foremost to create something of value, something that serves others. The provision of returns to investors is a consequential byproduct. Biographies and eulogies of successful business magnates focus not on the wealth they amassed, but on the number of lives they positively impacted through their entrepreneurial creations and the associated employment opportunities they provided to others, neither of which seemed to be as overtly celebrated up until that time, relative to the spoils of material wealth.

Deathbed clarity can be a cruel send-off that retrospectively reveals the opportunity cost of one's life for oneself and society. It is far better to sweep away the diversions at any point in time before then, to determine where one's life utility lies while there is still time to do something towards it.

In finance, the Entrepreneur and the Investor are the most legitimate stakeholders. Their legitimacy is underpinned by the value they create for society: one through generating employment, goods, services, and technology, the other by financing these efforts. Every contributor to a company's growth and survival can be termed an 'Entrepreneur', and anyone with personal resources to invest in others' actions can be considered an 'Investor'. Individuals can shift between these two value-originating roles throughout their lives.

Companies, more so than individuals, require money for survival. The more funds a company attracts, the more secure its existence becomes. Without funding, it ceases. Companies do not exist in isolation from people. Each individual that interacts with a company in various capacities – employees, investors, neighbours, customers, suppliers, and regulators – form its network of stakeholders.

What transpires when each stakeholder naturally seeks to augment their respective incomes?

Friction: inherent, natural, or systemic. The individual goals of stakeholders need to align, their only tenuous common ground being the entity's survival from which they all derive some form of benefit.

And what occurs when systemic friction undermines the integrity of a system?

Patchwork solutions. To counteract the conflict, an ever-expanding lattice of incentives is overlaid, aiming to reconcile disparate interests to achieve a common goal. However, eventually, these patchwork fixes can become more prevalent than the original fabric.

Centralised capital market structures are now beginning to grapple with the nascent paradigm of decentralisation, which heralds innovative approaches born in the digital age. At this historical juncture, it is critical to pause and re-examine why companies exist in their current form and scrutinise the implications for individuals, entrepreneurial activity, and investment within this structure.

Recapitalism seeks to highlight the commercial and humanitarian shortcomings of the conventional approach to profit-based ownership and centralised decision-making before outlining a new potential structure where corporate ownership aligns with revenue and investment worthiness is driven by a decentralised universal ratings system that democratises capitalism through influencing capital flows.

It is postulated that the ramifications of applying these systemic tweaks are potentially life-changing to all humanity, and conducive to the rising themes of social and environmental concerns to reconcile and flourish alongside expanding enterprise and industry. Simultaneously, the proposed approach creates a setting to practically humanise the concept of global capitalism by both opening opportunities to all investors regardless of location-based differences and returning the all-important and destiny-determinant sense of 'community' to internal company stakeholders.

Profound global movements are participant-led. The cry of 'Governments need to act now', implying that the responsibility for positive change leadership lies predominantly with sovereign state administrators, is misplaced. While governments have a role to play, that role is not to act as some form of benevolent dictatorship on social and environmental issues. Given the appropriate mechanisms, the direction and flow of global investment can be democratically steered by all participant stakeholders. All that is required is a fitting structure.

Each human life is equally significant. Consequentially the global amalgam of social systems carries an aggregate responsibility that does not cease at, nor justify preference and priority within, sovereign-state boundaries. Every individual engaging in transactions is part of the financial system, and the underlying blueprint should be drawn to serve all participants.

Capacity, speed, efficiency, and reliability provide the fairest criteria for merit-based comparisons between different conceptual capital market structures, each of which exists to serve the best interests of individuals either investing or receiving funds in the hope of gaining returns from the value generated by enterprise.

The increasing integration brought about by the digital era creates new possibilities for funding genuine commercial potential, and for every individual to access it directly without deference to the physical, legislative, and systemic boundaries that traditionally segment capital markets. To unlock the power and prosperity of the individual, the economic system should aim for the most direct, transparent, well-governed, and efficient link between ideas and implemented innovation for the entrepreneurs, as well as between financial wealth and financial returns for investors.

A revenue-centric, decentralised, and democratic approach to capital markets may provide the framework to rekindle capitalism's 'free spirit', extend its relevance, and ideally uplift the humanity that economic systems are intended to serve.

"We have the chance to turn the pages over..."

PART I

A NEW HOPE

*"We can write
what we want to write...."*

1. Unleashing Human Potential: A New Dawn for Global Finance and Investment

Each life is unique, and everyone has the potential to make a uniquely positive contribution. Deliberate global societal structural designs should acknowledge and prioritise these two fundamental truths and seek to optimise their fulfilment.

People have a communal nature, craving the experience of interaction across various dimensions: emotional, physical, spiritual, intellectual, and creative expression. The rise of online communities has fostered connectivity, granting individuals access to a virtually endless trove of information and enabling transactions at will. This has resulted in a burgeoning of commerce, where, in many facets, interactions have become increasingly direct. Goods are now shipped directly from manufacturers, bypassing traditional physical retail chains, services are rendered remotely, and, fueled by advertising revenues, social interaction has evolved into one of the world's largest industries.

This development has resulted in an expansive array of choices for consumers in any given area of interest, enabling an incredible diversity of quality, price, and user experience. Supply and demand channels have evolved from historically local, geographically bound markets towards a borderless, global marketplace. While communications and commerce have been fundamentally overhauled with the online age, several frontiers still lie ahead in transitioning conventional and compartmentalised approaches. This 'compartmentalisation' takes the form of geographic, cultural, edu-cational, or scale-based exclusions to produce insular communities that, while they might adequately serve the interests of their immediate stakeholders, the societal benefits that may otherwise accrue from broader participation are precluded.

Global finance and investment machinations wield profound influence, determining the price and availability of everything from groceries to houses, the remuneration people receive, the infrastructure and services available, and essentially everything that can be purchased with money. This influence naturally then extends to the associated non-monetary impacts of trade. One of the key enablers of the flourishing of global commerce is the explosion in choice – both in what can be bought and how income can be earned. Despite its flaws, the online community has been instrumental in dismantling cost, inefficiency, and exclusion barriers in various sectors, from social engagement and health to access to goods and services, education, remote working, news, and entertainment.

To date, many traditional approaches to finance and investment have simply been projected online, which has helped expedite rather than transform industry practices. The paradigm-shifting reinventive breakthroughs are still to come in utilising the technological tools available to overcome the barriers of participant exclusion that persist in capital markets.

Creativity is an innate characteristic inherent in every individual, a fundamental mechanism for appreciating human uniqueness. Commercial creativity is at the nucleus of finance and investing, and its application in growing businesses is inevitably fuelled by funding.

While a symbiotic relationship exists between the creator and the funder, many parasitic layers often intervene, separating the two entities. Historically, these intermediary layers have mainly been beneficial in creating and maintaining environments where commercial creativity and funding intersect. However, with the new technologies at hand, the merit of these traditional layers of intermediaries bridging the giver and receiver of value in commercial transactions is now under scrutiny.

Consider the expansive domain of capital markets.

What if it were possible to forge a more direct connection between the creators of value − companies -and the funders of value - investors?

Imagine accomplishing this at an exponentially increased speed, accessing deeper pools of capital, and matching a highly refined risk/return profile that fosters greater trust and transparency in the overall process. Furthermore, consider the scenario where participation in either of these two categories is open to all, irrespective of wealth or geographical location.

There are many inspiring narratives of individuals born into intergenerational poverty who, by a miraculous stroke of fortune, gain access to privileged opportunities and accomplish significant personal achievements. Some have then profoundly impacted the world, contributing to academia, health, arts, and technological innovation.

With around half the world's population possessing less than $10,000 in assets and 10% living in extreme poverty, it's clear that these success stories are anomalies. The vast opportunity cost embedded in this unutilised societal contribution, which is sadly the latent asset of individual human wealth, is striking. Imagine the positive ripple effect of unlocking this dormant global human creativity, expanding access to entrepreneurial and wealth creation through new inventions, employment, investment, and services.

In purely financial terms, since the late 1800s industrialisation has decreased the global percentage of extreme poverty from 80% of the global population, where it had been for millennia, to around 10% today. However, considering global population growth, the actual reduction in the number of people living in extreme poverty is less dramatic. This unfortunate reality indirectly affects everyone and is a significant constraint to global human progress, as the primary 'survival state' consumes an individual's mental and physical resources. In a state of poverty, individuals expend their energy on securing basic survival needs. Any leisure time is allocated to much-needed rest and idle distraction rather than progress and improvement.

In navigating the third decade of the 21st century, awash with information and distractions, the idea of reflecting on the more profound lessons of historical experience and the notion of 'standing on the shoulders of the past' seems to be overshadowed by a prideful individualism and a perceived moral and intellectual superiority dismissive of the analogous lessons of the past. Within this, the verbally virtuous often direct much of their indignation towards capitalism for the world's problems. Yet, capitalism remains the only proven system that, on a net basis, has shown time and again that it can generate prosperity, lifting masses from poverty and facilitating broad innovation that improves health, living standards, and experiences. Capitalism is "a real system" that is misapprehensively compared to 'idealist systems' that, when implemented, have become humanitarian and gross productivity disasters time and time again.

Capitalism is not utopian. Its success lies in its pragmatic recognition and accommodation of human shortcomings. It acknowledges that people are driven by fear and greed, prioritising their interests over others. The free market guarantees no outcomes but strives to provide everyone with choices.

The internet brought forth information and communication, e-commerce facilitated consumer choice and now, blockchain-enabled trust and confidence to transact. Trust is the linchpin that unlocks the door to true globalisation, potentially elevating the practicalities of the capitalist notion of 'freedom'. Through this new, technologically enabled approach, the era of insular investment communities laden with parasitic intermediaries that separate companies and investors from each other could be bypassed. If the hand dealt is wisely played, the dawn of an age where individuals hold power and authority to determine their path, and seize opportunities to enrich themselves and their communities, is on the horizon.

2. THE NEW ERA OF DECENTRALISED ECONOMY: WORK AND INVESTMENT UNBOUNDED

It might seem bemusing now to recall that the first radio newsreaders were obliged to don dinner jackets, yet this serves as a reminder that with technological shifts, the once meaningful protocols of the past are carried forward until their absurdity finally dawns on the participants and they are subsequently discarded.

Following the global pandemic, mainstream corporate culture has finally evolved from merely arranging physical business meetings through digital communications to actually conducting meetings digitally as the new default. Similarly, as the trend towards remote working intensifies, the logic behind expending time, money, and energy and incurring productive opportunity costs – not to mention the associated environmental footprint – is under serious scrutiny. Cultural inertia is the most significant drag on technological adoption. Many people berate the online experience relative to physical meetings, inclined to revert to yesteryear routines rather than embracing the possibilities of change yielded by the new technological tools.

However, the advent and gradual acceptance of wearable interfaces and remarkable advances in user experience through the emerging transition to 'spatial interfaces' will soon provide people with a far more immersive sensory experience for most commercial dealings in online formats than in physical settings. In time, the 'corporate traveller' might appear as ludicrous to future generations as the dinner jacket-clad radio newsreader does today.

Globalisation is a recurrent theme across all economic fronts, and given that economics, at its core, is the study of human decision-making, it invariably impacts everything. The Australian farmer's livelihood hinges on the culinary preferences of China's restaurant diners. A household's fuel budget is influenced by OPEC pricing decisions, which shape retail spending choices, affecting the businesses' owners, employees, suppliers, and customers and triggering a multiplier effect in an endless chain of transactions.

Information has been globalised, and commerce is on a similar trajectory, extending from bulk commodities to retail. Currency has been progressively globalising as the price of money and commerce is affected by the relative pricing of all national currencies. People are now witnessing the bumpy breaching of one of the last old-world thresholds as pockets of the mainstream population start moving from sovereign central-bank currencies to global digital currencies.

One of the key societal bastions of structural centralisation – enterprise funding – lags noticeably behind the forerunners of the globalisation movement. While some incumbents have adopted new technologies to an extent, there is a blend of unconscious and conscious resolve to perpetuate the existing centralised structures, which are fundamentally incompatible with the ethos of the decentralisation movement. The layers of disparate securities legislation, centralised exchanges, and insular finance communities continue to hamper the liberation of entrepreneurial financing.

This is unfortunate, as enterprise originates and supports employment, innovation, consumer choice and a meaningful part of life's utility value. With such core value points, society would be well-served to optimise these positive by-products in an accommodative and nurturing structure that bridges the current divides between investment monies and enterprise.

Ultimately, globalisation should increase each stakeholder's sense of freedom. Freedom of the enterprise and freedom of the individual. The freedom, not just where to live, buy and earn, but also how to live and operate. Geographical borders are increasingly less relevant for individuals, and those entities either inherently or deliberately confined by them will find themselves increasingly restricted compared to those who utilise technology to enhance their access to the noble, universally desired life elements of more choice, less cost, higher returns, convenience, and lower environmental footprints.

Whether intentionally or not, the power of technology is spurring entrepreneurship, investment, and employment on a somewhat tenuous yet steadfast journey towards liberation from the remaining legacy pre-globalisation confines. For the advancement of humanity, the present generation must strive to unshackle these fundamental societal cornerstones for future generations, thus facilitating access to as many opportunities for as many people as possible.

The premise that 'work' associated with human labour is tied to physical location was never challenged in the foundational economic models of past centuries. It was taken as a given, since no alternative existed. Today, however, the evolution of connected devices increasingly allows human effort to be 'digitally distributed' to the intended destinations, irrespective of physical proximity.

Over the next two decades, as digital automation continues advancing and people born in the 21st century, having grown up in the digital age, dominate the global workforce, future generations will likely discard the idea of 'work' being tethered to a physical location. Companies that insist on clinging to this increasingly redundant concept will face prohibitive competitive and social pressures.

The notion of 'living standard parity' varies dramatically in associated costs between countries. A sum of money deemed substantial in one country may be considered meagre in another. With a physical office that serves as 'the workplace', employers are bound to select employees from a limited pool of individuals willing and able to live within commuting distance. Employers are thus forced to accept a comparatively limited supply of individuals with the required skills and experience who meet the location criteria and compensate them based on that shallow labour market supply-demand intersection. Additionally, they may have to navigate legislative, regulatory, or cultural constraints, which form the framework in which they operate and compete against other jurisdictions that may offer more competitive resource advantages.

The scope of work that can be accomplished anywhere via a digital interface is rapidly increasing. Even traditional physical industries like construction, mining, and agriculture are adopting machine automation and digital-twin environments, enabling 'remote workers' – a concept that would have seemed unthinkable until recently. Nonetheless, due to cultural inertia, significant shifts often take longer than necessary to replace old ways, with stakeholder adoption always trailing imaginative application and technical capability. However, the sheer force of the associated financial efficiencies will eventually lead to abandoning outmoded habits.

Furthermore, at the cultural level, in the exasperatingly slow movement towards 'civility' – being kind to each other – which in recent decades was termed 'Equal Opportunity' and is now badged as 'Equality' in its current iteration, the next obvious culprit to be targeted is 'Location Discrimination'. The societal mindfulness that 'individuals are born equal' and the evolving technological tools that exist to engage human effort, irrespective of physical location, will serve as an increasing ethical and commercial dilemma for employers that remain wedded to location-based preferences in their recruitment criteria.

The same principle applies to financing entrepreneurship. Historically, investors have preferred domestic companies, which is understandable as people seek the reassurance of familiarity. Investors see the brands, and in many instances, they are also customers or employees or otherwise feel a sense of association that provides that requisite level of comfort in extending that relationship to an investment. However, in doing so, investors forgo the opportunity to contrast these local investments with potential prospects worldwide. Concerns such as disparate operating rules, the ability to physically inspect premises, and differences in language, culture, and time zone all contribute to the perceived risk of any potential investment. Yet, from a purely financial investment standpoint, these macro concerns, in isolation, should have little bearing on the future investment return.

As will be delved into later in the book, it is possible to foster a sense of familiarity between investment cases by strategically applying available technological advances. These can be relatively matched on a benchmarked risk/return basis, unfettered by the perceived distortions of geographically based influences, most of which bear no substantive relevance to the actual quality of the respective investment theses.

3. Trust in Transition: Centralised to Decentralised

How much time and effort is consumed by the inherent 'lack of trust' between transacting parties?

Unfortunately, 'lack of trust' is a given, as wherever it is assumed otherwise, there potentially lies the exploitative opportunity to profit from breaching that trust. The conventional remedies to trust deficits are 'controls'. The controls that 'patch' the lack of trust allow the 'transaction bridges' to be crossed. It follows that the controls must also be well-formed to optimise the efficiency of the transacting system.

Centralisation has played a key historical role in building functioning economies up to the present time. New technology has now surfaced, leading to a burgeoning awareness of what could eventually be retrospectively reflected on by future generations as a 'bygone era' where there existed a nostalgic notion of 'trust in institutions', in contrast with the age of digitally based 'programmed trust'.

Trust is invariably a relative concept in practice, positively correlated with knowledge through its perceived influence on predicting potential future scenarios. If an individual claims to have an intimate understanding of another person or an organisation, they develop a character construct and, consequently, a projection of how that entity is likely to behave in future. Trust is reaffirmed as long as the entity – person or organisation – acts within these anticipated parameters. Trust in this context is a forward-looking assertion that any new information about the trusted entity will not surprise the asserter. However, if that entity behaves outside the asserter's projected behavioural construct, it may lead to accusations of a 'breach of trust', resulting in the entity losing its 'trustworthy' status.

Entities, including individuals and organisations, perpetually strive to present their profiles to their target stakeholders, encouraging familiarity within the desired interaction – whether as a citizen, customer, financier, supplier, parishioner, patient, friend, or partner. In accepting these societal profiles, the stakeholders are generally asked to invest either their money, time, sovereignty, health, or emotions based on the understanding that the entity will respect this investment and act in accordance with its publicised profile. Acting in alignment with their stated profile creates layered precedence, reinforcing the perception of trust. However, if the entity deviates from its projected profile, the vested observers may exclaim disbelief at the unexpected action. Admitting a failure in judgment can be humiliating; however, it may helpfully lead to introspective inquiries into the true nature of trust versus its perception.

The uncomfortable truth is that trust can always be broken, as everyone, regardless of their protestations of virtue, is capable of anything. While constructing perceived towers of trust around companies and governments is comforting and necessary in a centralised society, it must be acknowledged that they are merely groups of people and, therefore, inherently fallible. They can never be absolutely trusted, only relatively so.

Historically, however, if it were not for the creation and contribution of intermediaries in capital markets sourcing and issuing money, the productivity of industry and the living standards of today would never have been achieved. Nor would the technology that has enhanced and improved lives in terms of health, comfort, and entertainment.

The organisation of regulatory and intermediary functions into centralised bodies is predicated on two key concepts from which all other principles stem: 'Trust' and 'Convenience'. However, in practice, it would be more accurate to say an 'adequate perception of Trust' and a 'relative Convenience'.

The fallibility of any economic system is exposed by its unintended systemic incentives. As temptation grows to deviate from the prescribed path, so does the likelihood that those incentivised will heed the call—it's human nature. Incentives tend to cater to the two most potent human drivers: fear and greed. Suppose the motivation to act per the 'trusted' profile outstrips the motivation to risk it, evaluated through the perceived risk-adjusted probability of punishment versus reward. In pursuing self-interest, an individual will likely stay within the course laid down by their trusting stakeholders. If an individual feels accountable to others, that alone is often a compelling incentive to uphold that trust which is further fortified when tied to personal financial gain.

However, a significant challenge, and an underlying destabilising reality, is that organisations, though they may endeavour to project a collective conscience, do not possess one. They hold merely the tenuous amalgamation of their constituent parts—their aggregate 'conscience'—comprising each individual's choice of actions within the organisation. Thus, virtue-signalling from organisations is restrained by their ability to maintain the unified direction of their components, especially when these individuals, like everyone is, are fundamentally driven by self-interest.

Thus, when an organisation's trust is broken, the 'collective conscience' mirage dissolves. While it is 'the organisation' that takes the brunt of the blame, the fault directly lies with those outlier individuals who, in pursuit of personal gain, diverged from the professed 'collective conscience' and breached the group behavioural boundaries, acting contrary to the welfare of other stakeholders.

Such behaviour is a human tendency, a pattern woven throughout history, and is guaranteed to persist under any future economic and social systems. The historical perception of trust is fallible; its fortification has only been enabled through an evolving patchwork of centralised regulatory endeavours to channel fear and greed, address each free-market misstep, and, hopefully, enforce rules-based order to align the behaviour of each constituent individual with the organisation's 'collective conscience'.

This perception of organisational trust constitutes the principal battlefield for the coming age, guarded by advocates of centralisation who fear displacement by decentralisation. Decentralisation focuses on direct interaction between the ultimate transacting parties: the buyer, intent on receiving a unit of value, and the seller, who holds it.

From a survivalist standpoint, decentralisation may be perceived as a threat to the very existence of centralised institutions. During these nascent stages of deploying new decentralised technologies, participants are observing the wielding of the perceived power of centralised incumbency, with its self-declared nobility, as it strives to withstand the rise of a relatively subdued, non-aggressive adversary effecting profound changes in financial transaction processes, without the need for their centralised input.

Resistance is one tactic for an incumbent faced with displacement, while adaptation is another. Centralised bodies have attempted to maintain relevance within the decentralised landscape by creating partly centralised ecosystems. However, as mixing clean and contaminated water only results in contaminated water, so is the pure essence of decentralisation tainted by the involvement of centralised bodies.

It is only natural that investors and companies will take time to adapt to new systems and continue to harbour some legacy fondness for old methods to the extent that they find solace in their lingering presence in the new system. Reversion and inertia will be fiercely employed as the inevitable twists and turns of evolving decentralised systems expose gaps that proponents of centralisation will seize upon.

However, much like technological solutions to the relevant user-experience shortcomings of two-dimensional interfaces for physical meetings, the decentralised community will rally like a biological immune system around these anomalies, striving to eliminate them. This should be embraced as part of the natural progression, rather than resorting to outdated fixes whenever inevitable hurdles arise in advancing the new system.

In principle, centralisation is counter to the spirit of the decentralised approach, as it transfers trust back to insular groups of people who can never be as transparent, efficient, or objective as incorruptible programming supported by everyone in the ecosystem who wishes to contribute. Moreover, decentralising aims to reduce the inherent collateral time, financial costs, and exclusivity that render centralised models comparatively uncompetitive.

Given a choice and in holding the centralised approach to account, the relevance of the foundational capital market pillars of regulatory bodies, central banks, exchanges, financial institutions, rating agencies, and financial media should all be questioned to the extent that the societal benefits of these functions can be decentralised. Theoretically, if a novel approach consistently delivers a materially superior outcome for participants—investors and companies—that approach will gain market share. Change can occur through either volition or necessity. The former suits forward-thinking pioneers, while the latter suits those who adapt merely for survival. Any established centralised entity can potentially flourish within the decentralised world, if they embrace it. Today's centralised bodies can constructively contribute alongside all other participants, provided they possess the acumen to accurately comprehend and adapt to the evolving environment that they aspire to remain part of.

PART II

Cashflows, Shares, Obligation and Discontent: Tracing the Fault Lines of Capitalism

We gotta make ends meet before we get much older...

Justifiable unjust

Disgusted and disappointed, a man went to the local city square to protest the government's participation in a foreign war. He caught a crowded bus home after joining the chants and applauding the speakers at the rally. A military veteran boarded the bus at a stop on the way, and he immediately vacated his seat for them.

4. Cashflows and Conflicts: The Dichotomy of Business Ownership

The perception of future cashflows defines asset valuation. An asset—any item with ownership potential—cannot produce financial returns either through operational revenue or future sale if it possesses no fiscal value to its holder.

The resultant cashflows measure the ebb and flow of company performance. Consequentially, the prospective assessment of future cashflows by interested parties is a fluid process. Each new piece of information on the company and any external occurrence could influence future cashflows. Simultaneously, companies require funding to generate, manage, and grow these cashflows. This finance can be generated internally or procured externally from another party. If obtained externally, such as via debt or investment, there's an associated cost, in present terms, for sourcing it from any particular provider.

Historically, the conception of a share likely occurred sometime in the early Middle Ages, long before the first public share offering by the Dutch East India Company, apportioning the promised spoils of its shipping endeavours to voyage funders.

While it's likely that various motives precipitated the idea of 'fractional company ownership', it is illustrative to hypothesise that the conceptual creator of 'the share' may have been a proprietor seeking additional funding for growth. Having exhausted their monetary resources but recognising the commercial potential, they may have evaluated their assets in considering how they might raise the requisite capital.

In this hypothetical historical scenario, the lateral-thinking entrepreneur realised that their prospective future cashflows from sales held an implicit current value. They then sought to persuade others to acknowledge this present value and transact based on this assumption. As the owner and sole employee, they naturally thought that the net cashflows would be the most suitable basis for the transaction. From their viewpoint, this provided the intended tradable asset with its fiscal worth, that asset being a percentage 'share' of the future net cash flows.

In simplistic contemporary terms, the historical dialogue might have unfolded as follows:

Entrepreneur: "Could you lend me $10 to fund the growth of my business?"

Investor: "What am I acquiring for my $10?"

Entrepreneur: "10% of the future net cash generated by my business."

Investor: "So you're suggesting that your total future net cashflows are worth $100 today. How much did your business make last year?"

Entrepreneur: "Well, nothing, that's why I need $10 now. I anticipate making $20 next year."

Investor: "So, if you continue to make $20 per year, it will take five years for me to recover my $10 from my 10% share. Why would I part with my $10 today for that?"

Entrepreneur: "Because from year six, you start to profit from your original investment, which I believe will continue indefinitely, and if I can someday sell my business, you'll receive 10% of the proceeds."

Investor: "Sounds reasonable; let's proceed."

On the surface, this seems like a straightforward and technically feasible approach between an entrepreneur and an investor. The entrepreneur has essentially sold a share in their company's future net cash flows. This concept is a core tenet underpinning today's capitalist system, and is the keystone of capital markets. However, there may have been another approach that could have served as the keystone on which to anchor the systems of financing human endeavour forever after.

The initial 'net cashflow-sharing entrepreneur,' and the trailblazing capitalists who followed their lead would have likely known their potential investors on a personal level. These investors may also have contributed to the company's management, given that mutual advantage would be served. Under these circumstances, the splitting of net cashflows seems reasonable. By being 'in it together', each stakeholder contributes their efforts, sharing the rewards in accordance with their percentage ownership.

But what happens when the investor base becomes passive and detached from their investment, where the only connection is financial?

The investor invests their capital seeking a return, and the company is looking for finance to ensure sustainability and growth. Distinct pools emerge—one from which management reaps their rewards and another for the owners.

The advent of public offerings of shares marked the beginning of a disconnect between the company's controllers and its owners. While both had a common interest in the net cashflows, the controllers (or 'management') had broader interests. They drew their living expenses from the company's cashflows, expanded their empires, fostered innovation, and hired labour, each involving expenditures that directly impacted 'the net cashflows'. The net cashflows, which are the funds left after everyone and everything has been paid, are of singular interest to those who only participate as owners.

Such a scenario, where multiple parties have varying interests, is ripe for conflicts, especially when some parties have various interests that clash with those with a singular focus.

It's fair and reasonable, and very necessary, that the executive shareholder and other individuals dedicating their efforts to building value receive compensation. Investing in research and development and covering day-to-day business expenses are required to generate profit. However, potential conflict among shareholders emerges when some owners are entitled to access multiple cash flow points in the company, whereas others are not. Simplistically, a dollar paid to the manager-shareholder as wages is a dollar of profit lost from the net cash flow pool, which could have been distributed to external shareholders.

Fast-forward to today, and the disconnect between a company's ownership and control has never been more profound. The world's largest companies have multiple exchange listings, and shareholders spread throughout the globe. The external shareholders have only a financial relationship by virtue of their ownership, and many are not even aware that they have an ownership stake, as their money is invested by an intermediary, such as a managed fund, or even layers of money managers that obscure the end investor's view of the companies they own and obfuscate any sense of influence on those companies.

Further compounding the disconnect is the layers of derivative mechanisms, each with its respective liquid market of buyers and sellers that influences the valuation of underlying companies, and yet are perceptively detached from them.

Capital markets, ostensibly about connecting investors with entrepreneurs, have grown into the world's largest industry, touching everyone through their far-reaching determinant influence on the price and availability of capital. People should understand what they own, particularly if what they own concerns other people.

5. Share ownership: The Concept, the Entitlement and the Conflict

Revisiting the universally engrained concept of the fractional unit of company ownership known as a 'share'. A share, from a perceived value perspective, is simply an entitlement to a defined percentage of the net cashflows of a company. That is an ownership 'share' in those cashflows.

'Entitlement' is a notion that warrants reflection in the contemporary context of share ownership. Entitlements should be something the owner can reasonably expect to receive should they wish to do so. However, an entitlement that the owner *might* receive, that is conditionally dependent on the actions and inclinations of others, is hardly worthy of being termed an 'entitlement'.

Two critical thresholds must be crossed for shareholders to tangibly receive their 'entitlement' to future net cash flows. The first is that net cash is generated from management's stewardship of the company. The second lies in the hands of the company's directors, appointed by the shareholders to 'manage the management' on their behalf. The decision to disburse the available net cash from operations to shareholders sits with the directors. To encapsulate more accurately what a share represents and the notion of entitlement, it could be more appropriately designated as a 'Distributed Net Cashflow Share'.

Suspending ingrained beliefs and understandings of traditional share ownership to revisit the first principles with an open mind, entertain a hypothetical dialogue between two fictional people, Pete, the entrepreneur and Mark, the investor.

――

Pete: "Fancy investing in my business? I'll give you a cut of my earnings after I've paid my bills and spent as I like. If there's anything left, I might decide to save it for later or give you your share of the leftover cash."

Mark: "So let me get this straight. I give you money now, and that entitles me to receive a percentage of your leftover wages, if there is any, and even then, you don't have to give it to me?!"

Pete: "Spot on. Do we have a deal?"

Mark: "Hang on a sec. What if I think you could be earning more, or I don't like how you spend it?"

Pete: "Well, mate, you can't tell me what to do with what I earn or spend."

Mark: "So I just have to trust you'll look out for me by trying to earn as much as you can, keeping your spending in check, then deciding to give me my slice of the pie?"

Pete: "I get where you're coming from. How about we appoint some folks to watch out for your interests? I'll report to them, and they can boot me out if they think someone else can do a better job with the cash."

Mark: "Ah, I see. So, by agreeing to this, we're admitting that we have different interests regarding the amounts you make and if and how it's spent and distributed. It's either all spent, or some of it comes to me. We're counting on these reps to keep an eye on you, and they'll decide whether or not to give me my share?"

Pete: "You've got it! And hey, if you're not happy with your reps, you can vote them out based on the power of your ownership share in my leftover cash."

Mark: "But if you own most of the shares, you'll effectively choose my reps?"

Pete: "True, but if they encourage me to make as much leftover cash as possible, that's good for both of us. After all, I get most of that, so I have a real reason to keep your interests in mind."

Mark: "Sort of, although you're more tempted to pocket the money through expenditures while still controlling it, as you have a 100% claim on that. I'm relying on these so-called reps to look out for me. What's in it for them?"

Pete: "We'll have to pay them for their troubles and the risk they're taking on your behalf."

Mark: "So their fees are another bill that gets paid out of the cash before it gets to me?"

Pete: "We could give them some shares. That would save cash and keep us all on the same page."

Mark: "But that dilution of ownership would mean even less cash is left over for me."

Pete: "If you don't like how things are going, you can always sell your shares to someone else."

Mark: "That's dodging the problem. I'm investing based on value, not just hoping to sell to someone else with a rosier view of the cash you'll make in future..."

Noting the simplification of the above in the context of corporate ownership, however, the intention is to highlight the inherent tension that exists between the objectives of a company's management and its shareholders. Setting aside their obligations to shareholders and acting purely in short-term self-interest, managers might aspire to operate at a near-zero profit to maximise their financial gains. This perspective also allows them to indulge in superior facilities, lavish travel arrangements, plush offices, and additional staff to lighten their workload as the surplus cash flow allows. Conversely, in seeking to maximise their financial interest, the external owners of a company harbour opposite aspirations for the company's expenditures. They seek to minimise costs to optimise net cash, which defines the value of their investment.

This dichotomy is less prominent in smaller companies, where the management and the owners often overlap, creating a significant degree of alignment. However, this divergence becomes more pronounced as the company expands, welcoming more external shareholders and employees.

Global for-profit institutions would have seemed implausible in the nascent stages of free-market systems. Today, however, the world's leading companies boast revenues and stakeholders—customers, investors, employees, suppliers and communities—that surpass many nation-state economies.

Due to a funding need at a particular juncture, and the issue of new shares to raise funds to meet that requirement, an executive owner relinquishes a part of their claim to these cash flows in perpetuity. Conventional share ownership is a blunt tool in this regard, with temporary funding needs mismatched with permanent changes in the capital structure, which impact all shareholders thereafter. Applying collars to limit upside and downside risk in share issues and ownership is sometimes possible. However, they require the use of derivative instruments or bespoke agreements to achieve it rather than being a feature of the conventional share.

The features of a conventional share have remained narrow and inert for too long. With the novel trust-enabling digital transactional tools now available, the nature of the conventional share must be scrutinised and challenged to ensure the universal funding instrument that it is, remains optimally fit for purpose. That purpose being to provide an efficient asset for the exchange of funding for investment returns.

6. Steering Profit: The Intersection of Ownership, Control, and Operation

It is pertinent here to take a brief detour back to the foundational principles that define what a company is, how it secures its financing, and the inherent characteristics of the key stakeholders, all of which are intertwined with associated systemic structural incentives, both intended and unintended.

In contrast to people, companies do not have an innate physical dimension. Their existence is a matter of legal documentation, but practically, a company comes into being through the lens of human perception, discerned through its observable manifestations. These encompass employees, products, projects, property and other tangible assets and their effects on other entities, individuals, and the environment.

Under the prevailing laws in any given jurisdiction, a company is acknowledged as a legal entity, sharing certain rights with individuals such as entering into contracts with other entities, and initiating, or being subjected to, legal action. Its creation follows a standardised registration process, overseen by the relevant government regulatory body that administers the local legislation for registering companies within a given jurisdiction.

Establishing a company universally requires a name, a registered address, an owner, and a controller. The owners and controllers are the primary stakeholders who effectively manifest the company's existence, beyond its official registration. These are the individuals with an ownership stake – shareholders, and those who control it by contributing their labour to it, namely directors and employees. Each typically seeks a financial return for themselves that the company's activities must generate. 'Owner' and 'Controller' are not mutually exclusive stakeholder roles, implying that an individual may occupy either or both concurrently.

By its design origins, the formation of a company bears parallels to the founding of a sovereign nation, where citizens agree to surrender certain liberties to a government under a constitution. Similarly, a company operates under core rules defined in a contract between its controllers and owners. This contract is commonly referred to as a 'constitution', 'articles of association', or similar terms of reference based on the relevant local legislation. It stipulates the core parameters and procedures the company must adhere to in its operations.

The owners, or 'shareholders', each possess a percentage share of the company's net cash flows, and aim to benefit from these net monetary gains resulting from the company's productive outcomes. The productive outcomes encompass everything the company generates, including services, products, intellectual property, and other units of value produced by the company's workforce and operational assets. The company then markets these units—its products, services, intellectual property or other assets—to generate monetary income.

There is a quintessential formula that describes the flow of monetary value through a company:

Income – Expenses = Profit

The magnitude of the positive outcome of this formula defines the extent to which the company has achieved a profit, that being the difference between all the costs it has incurred in its activities and the price attained from selling its wares. Contingent on the timing of cash receipts and payments, the surplus cash profit is labelled 'free cashflows'. The term 'free' suggests that these cashflows are more than those needed to meet operational expenditures, and it has its own version of the basic formula:

Cash In – Cash Out = Free Cash

When an enterprise requires financing beyond its internal capabilities to accumulate adequate free cashflows, it must seek external funding. Essentially, the company has two options: borrow money or sell an asset. Borrowing entails repayment, while selling an asset, depending on the terms of the sale, typically does not. Shifting the focus to the latter option, the company could liquidate an asset it owns, such as physical property, equipment, intellectual property, or commercial contracts, and realise the value of the sale proceeds. Otherwise, it may choose to sell a portion of its future net cashflows, commonly referred to as 'Equity'. As covered earlier, a 'share' represents a fractional unit of ownership of future net cash flows.

Competitive creativity for the provision of funding products in capital markets has produced an expanding array of conditional equity sales, including negotiated protections and advantages for both the buyer and the seller. Each variation of equity offering merely constitutes a 'derivative'. That is, it derives its inherent value from something else, that value ultimately being the ownership share of a company's future net cash flows.

The derivative market is a significant part of capital markets, and deeply influences the trading price of quoted equity. Derivatives essentially exist because shares are a static instrument – their nature is fixed, and they cannot be extensively customised to meet the endless tailoring to investor demand, prompting the creation of new instruments to be sold into the market. The 'future net cash flow ownership' encompasses both the cash generated from the asset and the money obtained from its sale, such as when the business itself—or a portion of it—is sold. This is a core feature of share ownership. As with any other form of ownership, the owner enjoys both the returns delivered from the asset as well as the return delivered when they dispose of that asset.

In summary, and notwithstanding the nuances that apply in certain cases, a shareholder is typically entitled to:

- A number of 'votes' on certain key company decisions, with that number generally proportional to their respective percentage ownership.
- Receipt of the net distributed cashflows owing to that share.
- The receipt of the sale proceeds when the share is sold.

Company ownership, control, and operation are typically structured in three tiers:

i) Ownership: Shareholders who own the company.

ii) Control: Directors who are appointed by and represent the shareholders and are legally responsible for supervising management to ensure shareholders' interests are optimised.

iii) Operation: The employees who manage the company.

In a small business, a single person may assume all three roles. However, as the company expands, different individuals may occupy each role. And, as with any aspect of life, increased human involvement leads to greater complexity and a heightened potential for conflict.

To illustrate the dynamics of company structure and its intricacies, a parallel can be drawn with an individual owning a taxi. The taxi is the sole operating asset of this company, and the individual is the sole proprietor. In the pursuit of generating their income, the person exercises absolute freedom in deciding how and where to operate the taxi and the choices regarding its maintenance, enhancement, and potential sale.

Now consider a scenario where multiple people own the same taxi. Since they cannot operate it simultaneously, the owners elect a representative to decide its operation, maintenance, and any necessary upgrades. Suppose the owners collectively evaluate the condition of the taxi and its operation and wish to replace the driver. In that case, they can do so through a majority vote, corresponding to their percentage ownership. However, suppose a certain owner has grievances against the driver, the other owners disagree, and the aggrieved owner lacks the voting power to effect changes. In that case, the incumbent driver remains in charge. The discontented owner's only recourse is to locate a willing buyer for their share in the taxi.

In this second scenario, the driver may just be an employee without an ownership stake. Their interest lies in maintaining the taxi so that it continues to enable them to derive an income. However, the owners are concerned with the net income after deducting all expenses. Along with the driver's wage, the expenses include taxi licensing, fuel, driver training, car maintenance, upgrades, repairs, legal fees, fines, tolls, parking, registration, insurance, and other items commonly associated with taxi operations. After deducting these expenses from their income, the owners hope that there is a net amount remaining. Assuming the driver has complete executive autonomy, the owners will need to trust that the driver will elect to distribute this net amount to them instead of awarding themselves a higher salary, making unnecessary upgrades, or simply withholding the money for potential future expenditures.

As the ownership base grows the owners elect a number of representatives to ensure the driver acts in their best interests. In this process, they place another layer of trust in these 'owner-representatives'.

The relevant regulatory authority broadly outlines and legislates this trust, which imposes core responsibilities on these representatives to act in the owners' best interests. These representatives are remunerated for their time, effort, and duties, imposing an additional cost and reporting burden on the driver and, all else being equal, further reduce the net income by adding to expenditures.

The primary focus on optimising the taxi's performance is diminished through the resource-draining complexities and differing motives of the various stakeholders with differing financial interests in the taxi's operation. The representatives might now attempt to implement a remedial 'patch ' in response to this potential 'conflict of interests' between the driver and the owners. This could involve offering the driver an additional incentive to maximise net income from their activities and salary, balancing their interests with the group. While this incentive could potentially dilute the owners' returns, the hope is that it will be counterbalanced by the incremental performance generated by the encouragement of financial self-interest of the employee. Adding moreover to the diminishment of focus, the driver must inevitably divide their attention between operating the taxi and adequately allocating time to report their activities and results to the owner-representatives and directly to the expanding ownership base and the regulatory bodies overseeing the representatives.

Stepping back from further specifics as the point here is to consider the overarching structural approach to company governance and its implications. For readers acquainted with existing corporate structures, this illustrative example, while appearing overly complicated for a sole-operator business, merely touches on the myriad of regulatory and incentive frameworks that have evolved to govern companies. If it is complicated for a taxi company, how much more so is it for a multinational corporation?

The elegantly simple theoretical underpinning formulas of accounting and economics quickly unravel in the subject community that tries to stitch them back together through every means possible. Any arithmetic taught to students that involves people in the equation must be explored further to appreciate its collateral behavioural, fiscal and social implications.

7. Capitalism's Chameleons: The Shifting Landscape of Rules and Incentives

Capitalism is not inherently rule-friendly. Often, the imposition of rules only leads to time and money being spent on achieving an optical alignment, while maintaining progress towards inimizing the incentive-defined objectives.

It is the incentives that drive the outcomes, not the rules. Fear disinclines action, and greed prompts it. Rules are only a backstop and a blunt inhibitor of action while also being resource-intensive to administer. Furthermore, new rules are generally created reactively, and thus are limited in their ability to regulate negative novel actions.

Incentives, however, are forward-looking and precipitate action, especially novel action designed to maximise the reward from the incentives. Incentives are part of the design, while rules correct the failings of the design. An incentive is an implicit and collateral or intentional consequence of the design. Rules are explicit and, in theory, exist to prevent an implicitly 44inimizing44d action that negatively impacts others. It is always better that the incentive structure is designed to align with the net benefit of all, 44inimizing the requirement for rules to address the design failings that serve to give oxygen to malevolent actors.

The progressive introduction of rules in a social system is symptomatic of a flawed incentive structure. Ideal incentive systems should reward actions that benefit all stakeholders, thus eclipsing the gains made by those who seek to profit at the expense of others unethically. This perspective should be the yardstick against which economic mechanisms are evaluated. Broadly defined, 'economic mechanisms' pertain to the context within which economic participants make decisions.

People respond to incentives. Incentives that they believe will increase their 'comfort'. Beyond the physical, 'comfort' is a feeling measured by the individual's perceived distance between general contentment and the loss of it. The feeling of comfort is akin to that of 'peace', a state in which one is not troubled by fear. As time is an egalitarian constant unaffected by individual will, peace begins with a sense of ownership over one's time.

The deficiencies in incentive planning in social engineering initiatives inevitably lead to the imposition of controls. Controls are explicit directives that stand between people and their objectives, which they otherwise feel incentivised to pursue. However, while the allure of the incentives remains, ingenuity will beat control every time, despite the overlaid controls trying to catch up by increasing in number and severity.

Controlling mechanisms quickly develop a paradigmatic existence of their own, as the controllers of the associated governing bodies recognise the means through which their own existence is made possible and naturally strive to survive by seeking to increase their received allocation of supporting resources and the pervasion of their reach. The raising of these resources and the consequent compliance of the subject stakeholders is essentially achieved and results, respectively, in diverting monies and efforts away from entrepreneurial activity to support and comply with the bodies that are charged with administering the controls.

The system perpetuates with each perceived failure of 'control' in its purpose of limiting or diverting malicious actors from their target, serving only to create further opportunities to promote the need for more controls. The best of human effort is more inclined to respond to positive incentives than to punishment, as the former provides scope for creative expression and reward while the latter prompts only the requisite minimal efforts to avoid the punitive stick.

It follows that, in the effort to optimally mould societal behaviour—as every organised group, from governments to companies, to social and environmental advocates, to community sports clubs is trying to do in a positive way from their perspective, while economising the resources dedicated to those efforts—that a natural starting point is to seek to correctly frame the incentives. Success will be measured by the extent to which the genuinely undesirable manifestations in society of unchecked entrepreneurial greed are economically disincentivised, to the point where the individual monetary rewards for activities that are aligned with the broader public interest exceed the incentives of detracting activities. That is, the reward for doing good exceeds the reward for doing evil in the context of a societal system.

However, ideological success in this endeavour will not be construed as 'a win' for all existing systemic stakeholders. What may make logical sense for society in general, with respect to structurally curbing malevolent actors, could be destructive for the regulatory industry that, sceptically though, when considered in isolation with a self-preservationist view, is founded and depends on continued wrongdoing for its justified existence and propagation. If there were no crime in a city, would that city require an expansion of criminal policing?

Nothing in life is absolute. There is no 'on or off', 'black or white', or 'A or Z' setting, it is always oscillating anywhere from 'B to Y'. Crime exists as there is an incentive to do it. If the incentive were not there, then it would not happen. Controls are necessary to protect people from violence in all its many forms; physical, psychological, social, spiritual, and financial. However, there must be a balance between incentives and controls, and that balance should first be achieved by the incentive framework inherent in the design.

In every possible sphere, and specifically in the context of the corporate sector, the participants, which ultimately is everyone, should look to the natural regulation of 'incentive' rather than conceding the unwanted behaviours and trying to play an inefficient 'catch-up' through the development, and enactment of controlling regulations and discreet enforcement.

Turning to specifically address the corporate sector and capital markets:

Who should be the judge of what constitutes unwanted behaviour?

Should it come down to small collectives of organised groups of people focused on specific subsets such as publicly funded regulatory bodies and for-profit companies, such as stock exchanges that are practically purposed by governments as quasi-regulators without true public accountability?

Can these stakeholders be truly trusted when once established, their incentive to survive through propagation may compete against efforts to change the underlying system to augment behaviour that is detrimental to society?

There is a significant ripple effect in establishing or removing rules. In one sense, rules can risk diminishing the humanity of the individual, as they promote conformity. Yet, there is also a perceived societal nobleness in following rules as people ultimately crave order which is a necessary underpinning to societal progress and peace.

Operating outside the rules is seen as acting against the interests of the broader society. Rules and incentives explicitly manifest a deeper driver that shapes them—the intriguing innately human quality, and one of the more profound and yet overt driving behavioural determinants: 'Obligation'.

8. Beyond Profit: The Morality of Business Purpose

While incentives and rules compel behaviour, the sense of obligation provides another lateral skew. Regulations and incentives are directly tied to the compulsions spurred by fear and greed. However, the manifestations of obligation are a step removed and resonate with a moral driver, a commitment, a duty that provides the ethical foundation supporting the execution of the 'appropriate behaviour'. The aggregate human imprint on the world is only the sum of its parts, and no individual should seek to conscionably diffuse their respective contribution.

For an individual to discern their obligations accurately, then determine the appropriate resultant behaviours, it necessitates a comprehensive and nuanced understanding of their responsibilities to themselves, their families, friends, the companies that they work with, shop with, and in-turn the stakeholders of those companies—employees, customers, suppliers, shareholders and so on. Moreover, each individual sustains a relationship with the broader society, the natural environment, the spiritual dimension and other driving elements.

If it is difficult for one individual to clearly comprehend their own collage of obligation and what they should do about it, how much more difficult is it to comprehend the deeper underlying drivers of others?

And yet it is imperative that those seeking to corral others, which most people are trying or hoping to affect in some sense, that they do.

Competing obligations have varying relative strengths in each person's perception. The most potent perceived moral obligation is always likely to be the one that guides behaviour. A sophisticated understanding of consequential obligation within a given behavioural framework is a key foundational reference point in analysing and predicting human inclination, and the resulting activities within that structure.

Consider applying this approach to the core traditional capitalist notion of the division of corporate ownership at the distributed net cash flow level. An asset exists at the pleasure and for the service of its owner. A logical presupposition is that the owners of the net cashflows are primarily interested in the progressive optimisation of their asset to fulfil its purpose, which is maximising its value. Put simply, shareholders care about 'shareholder value'.

In the marketplace, an asset's monetary value—a share or other corporate asset—is dictated by the buyer's perceived quantum of future cashflows, as it is only the future cashflows that prospective owners may benefit from. The prevailing adage is that 'businesses exist to make a profit', as first and foremost, the business is obliged to serve the interests of its owners. Expanding on the context of the previous taxi example, consider a sole proprietor that owns 100% of their business. At the most superficial level, the cashflows that the proprietor receives from the business may either take the form of wages at the expense line or net profits at the bottom line. Taxation and market value aside, and all things being otherwise equal, the maximisation of either wages or profits makes little difference to the benefits received by the proprietor as they are the exclusive owners of each; The sole taxi owner-operator receives 100% of any wages or profits paid.

However, as soon as another party becomes involved at the ownership level, the proprietor bears an obligation and is morally accountable to that party's interest in the business. The proprietor cannot then, as before, in good conscience, simply triple their wages as their new fellow owner, who only has an interest in the profit line, will directly lose value from their ownership interest in the form of the reduced net cash flow available for distribution. All things being equal, each dollar to the taxi driver is a dollar less potentially available to the new shareholder in the distributed net cashflows – commonly known as 'dividends'. The dilemma exacerbates as additional shareholders join the ownership structure. The scrutiny is such that the proprietor's ethical freedom regarding setting the expenditures of the taxi company is effectively curtailed due to the obligation to the other owners, as they are morally obliged to focus their efforts on the maximisation of the profit line to act in alignment with the interests of all owners, that is by maximising net profits.

The complexity compounds as the taxi service expands and hires additional employees. The proprietor may harbour altruistic inclinations to pay their employees above market rates beyond what is reasonably required to retain and incentivise them. Alternatively, they may have environmental or social causes that they wish to support from the business's gross revenues, such as upgrading their fleet to comparatively more expensive electric vehicles or donating to charitable causes. However, while morally noble to the broader society, those inclinations risk muddying the purity and primacy of profitability. Thus, they are at odds with the interests of their fellow shareholders, who naturally seek to maximise the monetary return on their investment.

While an investor might assert a desire to support companies that pursue social and environmental causes at the expenses of profit maximisation, they would not then be 'investing' in the conventional sense of seeking to maximise their financial return on investment. To the degree that such considerations decrease the financial value of their asset, they are effectively 'donating', which is, in essence, investing without the absolute prioritisation of financial return. Although individuals may have diverse inclinations towards non-monetary outcomes from their investments, maximising monetary returns is a common, directly measurable outcome and, as such, remains the only universal yardstick through which business investments can be contrasted and compared within the paradigm of profit-based ownership.

Reiterating the distinction between financial donations and financial investments. The former effectively becomes a 'social investment', whenever maximising financial return is not the primary motive. A financial investment, seeks to maximise financial return. Furnished with that return, the investor then has the choice of how to spend it, which may involve supporting their personal social and environmental causes. However, the destination, timing and amount of their donations are at the discretion of the individual and not the investee company. Despite the prevalence of overt corporate virtue signalling, very few investors are willing to sustain diminished financial returns from their investments in 'for-profit' companies. This does not imply that investors lack consideration for perceived socially positive non-monetary outcomes. Instead, it suggests that doing so creates a 'double-agency risk'.

'Agents' is the academic term for the company's management, as they are 'agents' of the company's owners. Firstly, the investor hopes that their investee company's controllers (agents) can produce a financial return from their asset (the company). Secondly, when contemplating broader societal outcomes, the investor would be placing additional trust in the same controllers to administer the returns from their assets in the quest for various non-financial results that align with the investor's social and ethical profile. This gives rise to a 'double risk' that the company's controllers can achieve both the desired financial and the non-financial objectives held by the owners, be they social, environmental, or otherwise.

Each person's worldview is unique, and any presumption of alignment by centralised bodies such as corporations is likely to be false and potentially offensive to their stakeholders, as doing so asserts rather than respects the personal nature of perspective. The pursuit of monetary returns has a sufficient universal commonality, since the receiver can then spend those returns as they see fit. The altruistic expenditure by companies on social, environmental, and ethical concerns is far more problematic. The investor is effectively being asked to align with the worldview of the company's controllers rather than their own. A company claiming perfect alignment with their shareholder's moral and ethical profiles is merely guilty of 'aggregated social engineering' in representing the controller's views as those of their shareholders.

Moreover, the value of intermediaries, such as financial advisors, fund managers and others that invest other people's money, is typically measured explicitly in monetary returns. Thus, the only 'obligation' driving the behaviour of these intermediary groups is the maximisation of financial return. Should one group decide to deprioritise financial return relative to their peers, they will soon lose their clientele, as investors redeem their investment to seek superior financial returns elsewhere. The interplay between the investor and the 'investor's representatives', such as financial advisors, imposes a double layer of obligation on the controllers of the investee companies.

First, from investors seeking a return from their investment managed by the intermediary advisor, then intensified by the singular focus of the intermediary doggedly pursuing sufficiently compelling financial returns to retain and attract investor funds from which they derive their income. In practice, there are multiple layers of intermediary groups with fund managers that invest in other fund managers, such that the relationship between the underlying investee company and the individual end investor is effectively wholly detached through the indirectness of that relationship.

Through this obligation to the company's owners, the profit-motive puts the executive morally at odds with expenditures not premised on maximising net cashflows. The primacy of the obligation of the controllers to maximise the owner's interests through maximising their financial return at the profit-level necessarily relegates other broader societal obligations to the periphery rather than the centre of their core strategic actions. Whenever the company's owners and controllers are not the same people, the profit-motive becomes the ultimate defining morality of the company's existence. External societal pressures on management to de-prioritise profits are unethical from the owners' perspective, as it would mean the management would be acting counter to their financial interests. It is up to the company's owners to expend their financial returns received from the distributed net cashflows of the company as they see fit.

Altruism with one's own money is noble. Generosity with other people's money, without their express directive, is immoral and akin to theft. For a company to morally pursue anything other than maximising future earnings, it must have an explicit agreement to do so from its owners. Practically, this would be documented as an amendment to the company's constitution or equivalent governing rules, such that it is clear what the actual purpose, or purposes, are of the company. This provides bona fide clarity to investors and prospective investors of what the company is obligated to do with 'their money'. Then they can make their investment choice regarding their membership.

However, amending a company's constitution does not solve the dilemma, as the potential diminishment of financial returns resulting from the pursuit of non-financial outcomes. The highly personal nature of each person's worldview makes it very difficult for the aggregation of purpose and expenditure of shareholder monies not directly tied to the universally common interest of the maximisation of net cashflows. Under the current approach to company ownership at the net profit level, it is likely better that the individual investor receives their maximum return from their financial investment, then separately determines and controls how much and to which directed purpose, donations are made.

Much of the collateral social and environmental degradation committed by industry actions is often sought to be laundered by the notion of companies pursuing the objective for which they were created. There is nobility in fulfilling one's obligations; as such, the profit-motive is held up as a virtuous pursuit. People working for larger companies are often pontificated to by their management superiors about the virtue of shareholder value and why they should, almost altruistically, celebrate their positive efforts to that end. Of course, there is a sense of ethical justification when one group accepts the custodianship of another group's assets on the understanding that they will apply their best efforts to seek to protect, grow, and return it.

If an entity is created for a specific purpose, then that purpose is an obligation. That obligation falls to the people appointed to control the entity. In making principled decisions, people need to consider the given parameters in which they are to make them. If they do not make decisions in accordance with those parameters and breach them, then they are not making principled decisions which, in doing so, compromises their integrity.

Everyone should innately care about maintaining their integrity checked by a well-developed conscience. As the proliferation of online platforms ensures that information on everyone's respective activities becomes increasingly abundant, broadcast and catalogued, the importance of maintaining one's integrity is paramount.

Unless a person's primary interest in a company is via their ownership, then the profit-motive is only a motive by obligation. Outside the ownership layer, the profit-motive is more aptly named the 'profit-obligation'. Those controlling the company's activities are obliged to make a profit in recognition of that obligation. Consequently, society at large, in seeking an appropriate contextual perspective for the actions of companies, also must recognise the logical sequence of activities that results between the profit-obligation and the outcomes of enterprise.

Many ideologically-charged contemporary commentators deploy numerous guises to compel capital market participants to act in ways the capitalist system is not fundamentally designed to do in its current form. The key friction point continuing to surface stems from the growing commentary that those in the capitalist system 'should not' concentrate primarily on maximising profit from entrepreneurial activity. With broad and increasing advocacy of social themes, the integrity of the primacy of the profit-motive is under threat and with it, the nucleus of 'why the company entity exists?' is placed in philosophical question.

The world's largest companies have more impact on more people, whether as a workers, consumers, students or investors, than they have ever had. This is well recognised, and the representative societal commentary expresses an insistence that is becoming a social 'demand' that companies aspire to become 'good citizens'. However, while the individual is at liberty to incorporate every positive virtue regarding their character and conduct that their free will sees fit to encompass, the company, while being a legal entity, is not a citizen, and it is beholden to its owners to do what it was created to do, and is required to do, under the prescribed rules of its existence: to make a profit.

While ever a business strives to maximise profits above all else, it cannot be genuinely aligned with each qualitative element that society may wish to see it demonstrate. However, if the company's controllers are not striving to maximise profits, they are not discharging their obligation to its owners unless they have an explicit mandate not to. If the concerns of the customer base, suppliers, regulators, or other stakeholders that influence the profitability of the company need to be addressed, then the controllers of the company will do this under obligation though only to the extent that it relates to the earnest pursuit of profit maximisation. The controllers are not otherwise obliged, or indeed do they have the ethical liberty, to direct the affairs of the company to address the concerns of those outside the ownership base to the extent that it may diminish the interests of the ownership base.

Pursuing profit may result in collateral societal damage, however, profitability is inextricably linked to traditional corporate existence. No one comprehending this foundational concept could criticise an entity for doing what it was created to do. "Companies *should* do this" or "*should* do that", in consideration of the interests of stakeholders that are external to the owners of the company, at the owner's expense, is commentary that companies are not fundamentally obliged, nor should countenance in respect to their obligations. Outside of legislative and regulatory directives, the company's activities can be morally directed only through the owner's explicit directives, consistent with and embedded in the official and publicised corporate purpose.

A morally held principle is not bona fide until it costs the expounder money, and investors will not generally accept lower comparative returns, especially investors that are investing other people's money and are themselves remunerated on the quantitative financial outcomes of their investment performance, as they have a double obligation to their investors and themselves. And so, the pursuit of profit maximisation must necessarily continue to prevail in capital markets while ever company ownership remains defined at the net cash flow level. However, if 'net' were changed to 'gross' in the last sentence, that could change everything.

PART III

The Currency of Existence: Time, Wealth, and Human Potential

"We're all someone's daughter

We're all someone's son....

9. Perceiving the Worth of Human Wealth

Much as economics has been constricted in the mainstream discourse to encompass monetary matters solely, 'wealth', too, has been erroneously equated with pecuniary gains. This familiar narrative suggests an irrevocable correlative link between financial prosperity, personal value, and satisfaction. While it is undeniable that financial wealth can afford the liberty to exercise choice regarding the application of one's time, it does not seem to easily map to the more elusive personal feelings of fulfilment, contentment and peace, which everyone inherently yearns for.

One frequently proposed definition suggests that a person can be deemed 'wealthy' when the passive income from their investments surpasses the amounts earned by their direct efforts. This premise implies disassociating an individual's effort and time from the income generation sufficient to maintain their reasonably desired standard of living. While this seems a plausible proposition in the quest for 'financial freedom', it also stokes thinking on the old adage:

What value does financial wealth hold when one departs from the world bereft of material possessions?

On reaching the front of the queue that every person is in, all personal items are left behind. What matters most to personal fulfilment is one's state of being throughout life's journey. While money might play a role for some, it rarely serves as the principal determinant.

Therefore, what constitutes an individual's 'wealth'?

What weightage should be allocated to the monetary aspect within this definition?

In practical terms, there is no clear, universal correlation between wealth and contentment, as proficiently managing one's life once equipped with ample material resources is far from certain. In the context of wealth, monetary assets that surpass one's minimum desired living expenditures only buys choices, leaving the outcomes subject to the wisdom of the possessor's decisions. From a philosophical standpoint, a person's wealth might be defined by 'how good it feels to exist'. Despite each person possessing a unique 'internal dialect,' and reasoning that identifies different paths, everyone is consciously striving towards their own sense of 'internal tranquility'. This aspired sensation's diverse and dynamic perceptive nature renders it elusive and enticing, and its pursuit essentially defines each person's life journey.

Numerous biographical accounts of financially affluent individuals often assert, either in candour or possibly to absolve the vague sense of guilt often associated with excessive wealth, that money does not elicit happiness. Faced with a broader array of choices, these individuals grapple with their respective journeys towards a desired sense of peace, contending with the additional stress of navigating through a multitude of options and the despondence of realising that financial prosperity is not the cure-all solution that those without it often presume it to be.

A recurring assertion proposes that one must disregard oneself ultimately to attain happiness, thereby implicitly endorsing another adage, "A life lived for others is the happiest one." An intimate understanding of another often cultivates a natural empathy that manifests into a genuine concern for their well-being. This empathy fosters care for their experiences, treatment, and aspirations. In contrast, dehumanisation leads to objectification, which diminishes empathy. The pragmatic and empirically driven company owner perceives the most valued assets as producing maximum output at minimum cost.

For instance, if an excavator underpins the revenue of a small business, the owners have a vested interest in ensuring its efficient operation for optimised productivity. While the shareholders, or the company's owners, may 'care' about the well-being of a productive employee operating the excavator, this type of 'concern' is solely based on financial gains. This is not equivalent to 'caring' about the person, per se. If the employee ceases to be profitable, the controllers must sever ties with them to fulfil their obligations to shareholders — maximising profits and subsequently 'shareholder value'.

As cold as it might seem on humanist grounds, under the obligations entailed in the profit-based approach to company ownership, management cannot be berated for lacking empathy towards their employees beyond that necessary to optimise shareholder value. As corporations expand, so typically does their workforce. For publicly listed entities, the ownership base similarly swells, as more individuals take an interest in the company's narrative and acquire shares. Given this sheer volume of individuals involved, establishing a mutual and genuinely empathetic relationship between an ever-growing number of shareholders and employees seems improbable, if not impossible.

Empathy generally compels people to consider a broader view of another person's situation before making decisions about their future, to the extent that they are obliged to, or can. Conversely, an absence of empathy narrows this viewpoint to that individual's employment for a singular, functional purpose. When this becomes purely quantitative, as embodied in the conventional and all-permeating 'revenue minus expenses equals profit' equation, the disconnect from empathy for the individual, seen merely as an 'expense' helping or hindering the pathway from revenue to profit, is complete.

Management-owned companies are a community where empathy and commercial enterprise can peacefully co-exist in the good conscience of alignment of interest. These businesses can exist to make a profit while also serving the interests of the people that expend their life energies on the business, as they are one and the same. In these generally smaller companies, where the obligation is circular with 'owner managers', the profit-motive is not necessarily omnipotent across all decision-making. It does not need to be, as the community of owner-managers is aligned in receiving benefits from the expenditures at the level of wages and staff amenities, as well as participating in the net earnings – dividends. While profitability is essential to ensure the company continues serving the owner-manager community, it is more a 'byproduct' than a priority. This community places greater importance on revenue, providing both sources of their financial benefit: at the expense line, through employee benefits, and at the net cash flow line, concerning the financial aspect of their 'ownership benefits'. The pursuit of maximising gross cash flows (revenue) as opposed to net cash flows (profit) opens opportunities at the expense lines to make decisions that might reduce profit, but could enhance revenue. This could involve various forms of investment in employees, such as higher wages, training, and improved facilities.

Alignment between stakeholders cultivates fertile ground for empathy. Where empathy thrives, there is greater scope to consider a more holistic sense of an individual's 'wealth'. In any organisational structure, the primary structural obligations determine individual empathy and wealth implications. Though it might appear commendable to advocate for businesses to focus more on the value of the individual, such reasoning must be commercially driven to avoid misalignment with the company's obligations to its shareholders.

Amongst business-savvy individuals, a well-understood principle is that a company should strive to extract maximum value from its assets, which includes employment contracts with its employees. In pursuit of this end, structures and activities that diminish the employee's humanity contradict this basic premise. When the individual's humanity is not valued, it is better to look to machine technology to replace them. As the advance of machine automation progressively consumes all programmable functions currently performed by people, it becomes increasingly imperative for businesses and individuals alike to realise and utilise the true value of 'human capital'.

11. Towards Inclusive Capitalism: Awakening the Entrepreneur Within

Every individual possesses unique creativity.

Those who state, 'I am a creative person,' might imagine themselves standing superior or at least distinct from the crowd. Still, such claims bear as much significance as an individual boasting of their ability to breathe. Creativity is not merely an individual trait but an intrinsic facet of biological and, particularly, human existence. This ubiquitous quality, consciously or subconsciously, is at the heart of each individual's problem-solving abilities, not just in their vocation but in helping them navigate life's numerous daily challenges and opportunities. Creativity and humanity are inextricably linked.

If creativity is a universal attribute, why do some individuals perceive themselves as uncreative?

The explanation lies within the boundaries that confine creativity, defined by awareness, capabilities, and inclination. While some might say, 'I am not the creative type,' this assertion denies the innate creativity embedded within every individual. Like a moral conscience, creativity may remain underdeveloped in some, but its existence cannot be negated. Without it, even the simplest of daily tasks would be impossible.

Every human effort follows an assessment of the situation and, through applied creativity, results in a consequent action. Creativity determines decision-making. Creativity takes mental effort, and effort tires. Mental, physical, and spiritual activity requires exertion. Through persistence, the person becomes 'fitter', and, with repetition, recovery and ratcheting intensity, the faculty—whether mental, physical, or spiritual—is strengthened by practice.

Recognising the continuous application of creativity in daily life is crucial for 'feeling human', and its uniqueness bestows an awareness of individual identity. The simple notion of awareness is the necessary first step towards understanding that any individual can apply their creative faculty to shape the world. An individual's unique creative expression is central to their identity. No two individuals have ever lived identical days or experienced the same thoughts at every moment. The celebrated philosophical proposition, "I think therefore I am", suggests a consequential idea: "I act because I think", implying that each action leaves an imprint on the world, testifying to the actor's existence.

Individuals who do not engage their creative potential leave the world to some degree impoverished, compared to what it might have been if they had applied their unique talents. The most significant opportunity cost for collective human progress is the untapped creativity of individuals. Those who have been able to realise, nurture, and express their talents for the betterment of others are likely to experience a significant stride towards the universally sought-after feelings of contentment and peace. Any material rewards that arise are incidental.

During their early years, children explore various activities with innocent wonder, believing that they can pursue any path that piques their curiosity. However, their innocent wondering tends to contract as they transition into adolescence. The perceived constraints of personal means and circumstances prompt them to focus more selectively on their future pursuits. Fortunately, many traditional location and resource-related hindrances are gradually being surmounted, courtesy of the opportunities presented by digital connectivity. Deterministic circumstances such as information access, education, commerce, and employment are less tethered to demography and geography than at the dawn of the 21st century, a trend destined to continue as technology and, more presciently, culture evolves, until these legacy barriers of opportunity are thoroughly dismantled.

Each individual is just that, 'an individual'. Individualism is uniqueness. There is only one of each person, and the aspirational challenge for society, and each individual, is to fulfil the optimal appreciation of their 'life value'. While the individual can observe, judge, rationalise, forgive, and reconcile their own standing at each moment in time through their innate dynamic self-assessments of mind, spirit and body, everyone else can only hear what that individual says and does, and cast judgement accordingly.

In commerce, being appreciated as an individual is the first step to being paid. In completing that transaction, each person must rationalise their busy internal deliberations down to communicated words and existential deeds. Most deeds arise from an invitation, since only some dare to appear unbidden. However, when presented with a compelling opportunity to act, individuals are typically inclined to seize it. The invitation imbues a sense of obligation, compulsion, and entitlement that drives action. The ideal societal structure is one where a myriad of doors of opportunity are open to as many individuals as possible.

One of the most significant opportunity costs in optimising collective human welfare is the exclusivity of global financial systems that separate investors from entrepreneurs. 'Entrepreneurs' and 'Investors' are the two most valid stakeholders in finance, given their contribution to societal value: the former through their efforts in creating employment, goods, services, and technology, and the latter through financing those endeavours.

Regrettably, the term 'Entrepreneur' has been pigeonholed, often seen as the exclusive realm of a select few unique individuals endowed with innovative ideas, tenacity, perseverance, and financial backing necessary to establish and expand a business. This narrow perception of the term causes many individuals to dismiss their potential entrepreneurial traits, suppressing latent creativity which is an incredibly significant opportunity cost for society as innovation fuels advancements in health, wealth, entertainment, and overall life experiences.

Entrepreneurs require assistance to succeed, as their aspirations must resonate and inspire others. Those providing this support through their efforts should see themselves and be recognised by society as entrepreneurs. After all, individual accomplishments are almost always the product of team effort. Anyone involved in the production process is, in fact, an entrepreneur, as they contribute to the collective human endeavour.

Ideas hold societal value only if transformed into action, with applied creativity necessitating comprehensive and sustained effort. The conventional distinction between business innovators and employees must fully recognise both parties' contributions. Regardless of their technical, sales, administrative, or financial role, each person is integral to the productive venture. While the original innovator may initiate the project and continue as the recognised leader, developing an idea into a tangible success story relies on the team's combined creative efforts and achievements.

Individuals require a certain income level to sustain their perceived baseline subsistence comfort. This baseline varies considerably depending on personal circumstances, perceptions, and the standard of living to which they have become accustomed. It is a sad irony that the stress associated with securing one's desired subsistence level can obstruct the elevation of their creative faculties. The fear of risking their comfort can often shelve the means to elevate it. Becoming aware of one's creative potential, and mentally disconnecting from the daily routine to exercise this faculty for other purposes, is easier said than done. Every individual possesses creativity, and given the opportunity, the necessary time, resources, inclination, and effort, they can contribute to the betterment of humanity.

Even if not the original instigator of a venture, an individual with the desire and energy to support the creator's aspirations, with either time or money to invest, can become an integral part of the process. It is the combination of creativity, time, money, inclination, and effort—in whatever ratios they are endowed—that equate to each person's means.

Identifying an idea or opportunity is not the final destination but the initial stepping-stone to cross a vast river. The means to act on the idea are required to prevent it from being abandoned. These means are both internal and external to the individual. A person's internal means provide the spark of creative origination, which then requires the external means to manifest it. The affirmation, "If I want to do this, I know there is help available. Therefore, I am inclined to pursue it," encapsulates this dynamic.

Many inspiring stories abound of individuals who have dramatically altered their life trajectory to accomplish remarkable feats after receiving a substantial boost in one or more of the five core productive elements—creativity, time, money, inclination, and effort. Yet, considering everyone is innately equipped to be an entrepreneur, the number of people associating with that profile remains low. This number could increase substantially if the paths to entrepreneurship were made as broad, transparent, direct, and accommodating as possible, instead of the typically obscure, winding, and treacherous trails that prospective candidates have traditionally been obliged to navigate.

11. Temporal Economics: Unravelling the Human-Time-Money Trinity

Time is the great leveller, and money is the great differentiator. Contrary to the saying, time is not money. It never has been, as, unlike monetary assets, time cannot be replenished.

Typically, income can be generated by selling time, products, access, or money itself. The 'time' sold pertains to an individual's mental or physical exertion, while 'product' refers to the tangible results of such labour. 'Access', on the other hand, signifies granting the usage of an asset to another party, and 'money' concerns the charges for providing monetary funds in various forms, encompassing interest, fees, commissions, and returns on investment from capital growth and yield.

A sad reality in the context of human worth is that most of the global population derives their income from selling their time. The dilemma with this approach is that individuals are forfeiting their most valuable asset, a non-replenishable asset—time—which, once spent, signifies a depletion of their existence. For some, this expenditure may deliver all the qualities that lead to their contentment and peace. For many, though, it does not.

Those fortunate to have a long life have likely experienced the loss of someone close—a partner, family member, or friend. Often, it's through loss that one gains the keenest understanding of the value of the departed beloved.

Imagine if it were possible to reclaim just one day with that person. What percentage of net wealth would one be willing to sacrifice for this opportunity? One per cent, five per cent, ten per cent, or even more? The result of this hypothetical calculation, when divided by the hours in a day, provides a faint contemplative indication of the hourly worth of a person's time, viewed from the perspective of a loved one.

Well, may one cringe at the vulgarity of equating the moments of a loved one's life with monetary value, yet that is the provocative point. Is it then a great leap to ask if that person was an employee, and if so, what did they get paid per hour? In respect and acknowledgement of their life and talents, what monetary sum was allotted in return for each hour they gave? Did that fairly reflect their personal worth?

If not, why did that person labour so? Why was that the agreed monetary compensation? Most likely, supply and demand dictated it. There was an offer at that amount for a certain profile of candidate, and, in a competitive marketplace, that is the hourly rate that the person was able to secure and thus willing to accept. What hourly rate would a person accept if they knew that they only had 24 hours left to live? It is difficult to price, given there would be so many competing activities for their remaining time, not least of which would be spending time with the ones they love, as well as doing the things that they love?

What about a week? If their job was a significant source of joy, they might accept a specific monetary amount to dedicate a few hours in their last week to conclude particular tasks to leave a legacy. Nonetheless, most would likely still decline. How about a month? Within such a timeframe, if they lacked sufficient savings, they might need to earn a certain amount to maintain their livelihood and partake in their desired experiences before departure. Now, extend this contemplation to five years, ten years and beyond: to 40, 60, 80 years, or however long an individual reasonably expects to live.

Living with the certainty of eventual demise offers a grounding perspective for appreciating the finiteness of time and assigning an appropriate value to it. However, the precise moment of one's natural demise remains an enigma, such that no one can ever assuredly reconcile their short, medium and long-term life plans against their remaining time. The end of this curiously reversed 'diminishing returns' curve, where one starts with all there is and ends with nothing, cannot be easily plotted.

There are no other personal assets like time. The law of diminishing returns assumes that the asset can be accumulated. A person valuing a single day less than they would if it were their last one, under the perception that they have thousands of days ahead of them, is just what people do, though is it really sound reasoning? Life is for living. If a person were going to live forever, they could take it less seriously.

Every person that has ever lived —and will live—is a partner, family member and likely a close friend of others. When their time is spent, it is gone forever.

How can an appreciation of this be instilled in an economic system while still maximising the productive output of all available and willing human capacity?

The exchange of time for money establishes a finely tuned balance, permeating communities from the most deprived to the most prosperous. Individuals are impelled to expend their earnings on goods and services essential for survival, depleting their income and assigning their remaining time to the continued generation of the requisite monetary inflows. People who genuinely derive the greatest life utility value from their labour efforts may be convinced of their own contentment. However, that is not the case for the majority that, and often very consciously for the most part, 'work to live'.

In the top percentile of financially wealthy individuals, not one of them derives the majority of their financial wealth from the direct sale of their time. That is, they make their money independent of their time. For those that can, the most time-efficient way to make money is by investing money. Decoupling one's time from one's income is the first step towards financial wealth. As the lead indicative measure of everyone's perceived existence, time should ideally be appropriately prioritised by each person, and the societal structures people live under. Every individual feels it personally, though the perceived worth of other people's time generally diminishes in correlation with the level of direct personal connection.

From the previous chapter, it is an unfortunate general observation that, once the personal connection between Person A and Person B is diminished to monetary value only, then the richness of the human worth of B to A is all but non-existent.

Every person is an individual. Thus, their time is also unique to humanity. No person's time is directly interchangeable with another's. While this premise may seem to fly in the face of process-driven jobs where each person follows the same set of rules to deliver the same outcome, it is these jobs that will be replaced by machine automation in the coming decades, such that the unique humanity of the individual will be their greatest selling point when competing with others and machines for employment.

What is left for people is what is best for people—creative expression. Both originating and supporting it, the instigation and the rewards of which are uniquely human. To optimise human worth and potential with respect to the finiteness of time, a core goal of any modern would-be economic system, should include the pairing of the uniqueness of the individual with the agility of the machine and aspire to offer an environment that provides for the optimal productive performance of each.

PART IV

THE NEED TO REIMAGINE INVESTMENT: TOWARDS A MORE INCLUSIVE CAPITALISM

"How long
can we look at each other

Down the barrel of a gun?....

12. Personification of Profits: The Human and Corporate Dichotomy

Moving on from the selective observational comments on the human condition in the preceding chapters and returning to the challenge of reconciling the respective existence of 'the human being' and 'the company'. Attributing personhood to corporations is a precarious endeavour. When babies are born their parents are given a birth certificate. When companies are 'born', a 'birth certificate' is all there is. Any attempts to internally fabricate or externally superimpose human characteristics on a company are misplaced, as it only distorts its defined purpose, a purpose enshrined in its existence which is to act in its owners' best interests. This means profit maximisation in the current corporate milieu, where the distribution of net cash flow—or profit-based ownership—prevails.

What would society's reception be towards a person who prioritises financial profit above all else as their raison d'être?

Irrespective of any attempts to masquerade under a facade of greater social empathy, the drive for profit maximisation must pervade all corporate activities, as the corporation exists to fulfil that goal. As companies have expanded into global conglomerates, and their impacts on society and the environment have grown more consequential, demands for corporate social responsibility have intensified.

Nevertheless, companies can legitimately assert that they are merely fulfilling their purpose and, as such, cannot be rightly chastised for carrying out what they were designed, and expected, to do by their owners: maximise profits.

Assuming all other factors remain constant, for a profit-driven corporation, the rational evaluation of the owner concludes via simple arithmetic that all expenses should be minimised and revenues maximised to optimise their return on investment. Consider a narrow clinical biological assertion that human life is fundamentally about acquiring and consuming sufficient food, preserving bodily health for as long as possible, and perpetuating the species. In this context, such a perspective could be seen as a markedly reductive view of human life and its potential contribution to society. Various philosophical perspectives explore the meaning and value of human life, and reassuringly, most converge on the conclusion that life extends beyond mere biological existence for the individual experiencing it.

Similarly, if a company's touted values and mission statement were to be reduced to 'making a profit', it would likely fail to inspire a talented workforce to devote their time and energy to such a one-way cause. Similarly, it would fail to attract customers, leading the company to fall short of its self-serving vision and, ironically, not ultimately make a profit, much like an intentionally greedy, selfish person will probably find it hard to make friends and live a 'poorer' life as a consequence.

The true and enduring merit of the profit motive lies at the cash level. A human analogy can be drawn here, though only within a biological context. Just as an individual who neglects their need for food and water will eventually experience organ failure, so too will companies fail that never turn a profit. They will eventually run out of existence-supporting cash and cease to be. However, human tendencies often push extremes, leading to the perception of profit maximisation as the primary purpose and action of corporate entities. Consequently, that becomes an expectation of the owners, with all the other internal stakeholders obliged to deliver it. Theoretically, should this paradigm shift, and companies become officially absolved from the obligation of maximising profits, the pervasive concept of profit maximisation might be reconsidered, leading to an exploration of what 'corporate optimisation' truly means.

With average life expectancy nearly doubled since the start of the previous century, there is a growing and understandable global preoccupation with correlating the quality of life with its duration. Elixirs and activities related to the health of the mind and body dominate the information landscape, as it is a shared interest of utmost importance for all of humanity. With this unprecedented focus on the holistic welfare of the individual, it is similarly conceivable—and there are many encouraging signs—that the 'health' of the company will also be increasingly broadly defined.

However, it isn't easy to fit and apply that lens to companies while the obligation of profit-maximisation notionally permeates a company's existence. Without addressing this core notion, the case for companies to adopt a broad-spectrum view of their existence may continue to pervade the media, however, it will not decisively bridge the motivations of shareholders and their obligated agents.

13. Market Distortions and the Inequity of Capital Raising

To chart a course of societal change from 'how things are' to 'how things should be', one must first develop a robust understanding of the active forces of supply and demand, which underpin the fabric of any economic system. Competition emerges organically in an ecosystem where resources are finite and human desires tend to converge. The victor, in any free-market competition for limited resources, is the one who can outbid the rest. Consequently, the designer's comprehension of supply and demand dynamics becomes crucial for any system created for people to transact within. Their foresight can help to minimise systemic flaws, reducing the subsequent need for remediation of unexpected collateral damage.

Economic theory is hinged upon the principles of supply and demand, with the market price of any tradable item ideally set at their intersection point. A scenario of abundant supply and limited demand depresses prices. In other words, when sellers outnumber buyers, the reduced competition allows buyers to negotiate lower prices. Conversely, strong demand, coupled with limited supply, escalates the cost. This rudimentary academic concept assumes that buyers seek the lowest price and sellers the highest, as financial self-interest drives each party. This assumption is a keystone of market economies. Even for those familiar with the first principles of economic theory, it is always worthwhile pausing to contemplate the principles of supply and demand before engaging in consequential modelling.

A first key premise is that, as the number of able and active participants engaged in any given marketplace increases, the interaction of supply and demand in setting the price is increasingly optimised for those participants. Consider a market with one supplier and two buyers. The first buyer willing to match the supplier's nominated price would determine the price. If there are two suppliers for one customer, the price will decline until one supplier abandons the transaction. Introducing a second supplier or customer would naturally attenuate pricing volatility, given the increased competition that helps stabilise the market-driven price action.

This elementary principle forms the foundation of competition laws that sovereign governments gradually develop and enforce. These laws are enforced when market participants are perceived to possess excessive power, distorting competitive price-setting by the 'free market'. Such legislation aims to disfuse the influence of power concentration in market price setting. The existence and enactment of these corporate competition laws presuppose that maximising the number of parties on each side of a given market transaction optimally fulfils the spirit of competition legislation, measured by the extent of consumer choice in product and pricing.

Foreign exchange transactions constitute the majority of the world's transactions, which some might argue highlights the dichotomy of the increasing globalisation of commerce, constrained by the sovereign nature of fiat currencies. Following that, among the most common transactions is trading money for the future cashflows of enterprise and the derivatives thereof. That is, buying and selling shares in companies, and the layers of financial instruments that have their ultimate root value in those cashflows.

Whenever supply and demand intersect, it implies a balance of the two price-setting forces at a specific price point. In contrast to other economic systems, capitalist ideology promotes the unimpeded functioning of supply and demand in commercial transactions. Thus, any mechanisms restricting supply or demand can be seen as incongruent with the ethos of 'capitalism,' and its commonly associated catchphrase 'the free market'.

The effectiveness of supply and demand forces is evaluated by the fairness of the price they set, compared to other non-market-determined valuation methods, such as the discounted cash flow method, which provides a formula-driven present value of the company's future cashflows discounted for risk. This evaluation is, in theory, bestowed by the natural market-pricing actions of capital markets through the continual assessment of future cashflows, represented by the current share price.

'Market efficiency' is the yardstick for valuation. At its core lies information efficiency, which is influenced by the speed, completeness, and accuracy with which a relatively perceived 'truth' can be established, notwithstanding the subjective nature of this 'truth'. The theorem of efficient markets contends that, at any given moment, all relevant information is incorporated into a company's valuation, thus providing an accurate market-bestowed value for that company's traded shares. This idealistic benchmark has fostered layers of industries within capital markets intent on exploiting its imperfect application. However, to date, the notion of efficient markets has had sufficient merit, in practice, to underpin the functioning of capital markets.

The legislative frameworks, rules, recommendations, expectations, and other guidelines that govern capital markets are all rooted in the pursuit of market efficiency. This is particularly evident in regulations concerning disclosure, which mandate companies to provide the public with timely and pertinent information. Such measures aim to minimise asymmetric information between market participants, an issue that could be unjust, disruptive, and ultimately detrimental to a well-functioning marketplace.

Assuming that 'truth' can be quantified, all relevant information concerning any assertion should be reflected in a company's valuation. Thus, a crucial tenet of efficient capital markets is that investors can choose to be as well-informed as possible. This 'choice' pertains to the individual's freedom to consume and act upon readily available information. The timely availability of this information in an accessible form is vital for marketplace facilitators to fulfil their obligations.

Securities law in developed nations embodies principles concerning market-sensitive information. Securities is a general term for any financial instrument— shares, bonds, or instruments that may convert to shares rights, options or debt—that a Company may offer investors. It is generally illegal for parties to trade in quoted securities if they possess knowledge that has not been publicly disclosed, and that a customary investor would reasonably believe would cause a significant fluctuation in those securities if released. This legal framework echoes the concept of 'fairness'. If Party A, armed with undisclosed information, is aware that the share price will rise tomorrow and buys shares from Party B, who is oblivious to this, any profit that Party A makes the next day equates to a loss for Party B, who could have made that profit had they possessed the same information.

A straightforward, but not always apparent, reality is that, upon retrospective analysis, every trade has a victor and a loser. One party profits while the other loses, depending on the subsequent share price movement following the transaction. Legislation around undisclosed market-sensitive information suggests that lawmakers seek equity, in terms of 'equality', or simply 'fairness', in maximising the timeliness and completeness of information availability. However, beyond the overt actions prohibited by law, there are subtler instances where information and access imbalance persist in skewing market efficiency to the detriment of broader society.

Interest rate pricing by central banks and, separately, institutional investors' large-scale buying and selling sends deterministic shockwaves through capital markets. It can be challenging for individual investors to access the same information that institutional investors have, not so much about their investee companies but more about their own market-distorting actions. Major institutional portfolio re-weightings can trigger significant fluctuations in the affected companies' share prices that ripple through the sector and even precipitate global market moves.

The subject companies could be as oblivious to these external moves as the rest of the market. There is generally no requirement for 'timely' disclosure by the instigating party, barring substantial holding notices, which are only mandatory after the trading action has been completed and the share price impact has already been felt. This is a consequence of investment concentration. Suppose a company has a high percentage of its quoted shares in the hands of institutions. In that case, significant trading by these institutions will impact the share price, and minor holders will witness corresponding fluctuations in their investment value.

Proponents of the status quo may point out that the institutions exercise their respective rights to buy and sell following the rules, like any other investor. While this is valid, the result is that a small number of larger groups dominate the influence on company value and, consequently, the value of the asset held by all investors.

When a person becomes aware of influence, they generally respond to it. In the concept of companies, the executives within feel beholden to respond to the larger shareholder's requests for personal briefings and meetings. Notwithstanding regulatory attempts to insist that the material content of these communications is made public, this communication access inevitably leads to a skewing of information in favour of these larger holders. Although serving the larger 'investor customers' seems commercially sound, the institutional investors are not there in an investor capacity to 'give' something to the company, they are there to 'take', that is, to maximise their return like any other investor, and they are naturally seeking to utilise their scale to their advantage. Fundamentally layered in the decision-making is that the institutions have their own investors to which they are beholden, and the executives of the investment institutions are remunerated based on their periodic financial performance.

There are still some prevailing legacy notions in capital markets that institutions offer a higher pedigree of money for companies, given their sophistication as investors and the depth of balance sheet to invest, and thereby, at the extreme presumption, claim a sense of nobility in helping other investors through their 'very presence' on the share register. This notion is false. The returns of most institutions over the long term underperform the broader indices. All their expended efforts and deducted fees return their investors less than if they had placed their money in the major market indices that simply plot the unmanaged average movement of the constituent company share prices.

Transaction fees are another major contributor. There is a misaligned relationship between those that earn their income from the value of the parties involved in the transaction, and those that earn it from the transaction. In capital markets, there are two key fee streams: brokerage on the trading of securities and commission on the issue of securities. Most institutions have exposure to both, and each is incurred at the expense of investors. The former directly and the latter indirectly. When investors trade in quoted securities, they typically do so through an intermediary facilitating this service. The investor willingly obtains a service and pays the price accordingly, so there is no concern on that level. However, the investor is paying for that service to make money from the investment. The service provider, however, has no direct self-interest in what happens post the transaction—they are interested in the occurrence of the transaction itself. Therefore, their direct incentive is to conduct as many transactions as possible.

Fees for capital raising are charged as a percentage of the money raised, which the investor indirectly pays, as their investee company must cover these costs. Again, the interest of the broking institution in regard to their commission is maximised from raising as much capital as possible. However, existing shareholders face value dilution due to the issuance of more securities and the capital raising expense, which reduces the asset value of their investment. They must then rely on the company to generate a return on the funds raised that covers this cost, and is net value accretive on a per-share basis. Unlike the investor, the broking institution essentially has an each-way bet. Should they hold shares in a company that performs well, the value of those shares increases, yielding a capital gain.

However, if the company continues to rely on external funding, the broking institution garners additional income from future transaction fees. These two outcomes are far from mutually exclusive, with many companies growing in value while relying on external funding to fuel this growth, benefiting broking institutions on both fronts.

When a company's shares are traded on the market, the company's cash holdings remain unaffected, as monetary value is exchanged between buyers and sellers. However, during a capital raise, the company issues new securities and receives funds from investors, directly impacting its balance sheet as the amount of cash held and the number of shares issued increases. The anticipation of capital raises can stir investors to sell down their holdings to partake in the capital raise, or halt buying, since capital raises are usually priced at a discount to the prevailing market price—so why buy on-market?

Aware of this, investors naturally hesitate to purchase shares before an anticipated capital raise, perceiving that they would be paying a premium for the shares. Such selling activity, coupled with reduced buying activity, inevitably leads to a lower share price, and then the capital raise is completed at a discount to this share price. Companies that are alive to this often aim to conduct capital raisings when their shares appreciate, possibly following positive market disclosures. Investors holding through these periods must endure the induced volatility in the value of their asset as these games play out.

Three theoretical improvements might reduce this volatility: first, providing ready access to funding at a publicly known price at every point in time. Secondly, enhancing transparency regarding information availability for all investors. Third and most divergent from the status quo: diversifying and increasing the available funding sources. While some may argue there is already a significant diversity of funding in capital markets, many disconnects still need to be addressed when considering the global pool of enterprise, people, and collective financial wealth.

Investment institutions' ability to earn income from transaction fees stems from their systemic bridling of supply and demand for capital. The prevailing system allows institutions to invest rapidly in companies when needed. While this may seem efficient, it actually supports a de facto collusive pricing system, maintaining industry standards that create restrictive bottlenecks for the available 'cost of capital'.

Why is this so, when the company is ultimately offering an opportunity to individual investors?

If investors want to take up that opportunity, they will invest, if they do not, they pass. All things being equal, the individual investor nor the company has a beneficial interest in the fees earned by the intermediaries. Theoretically, if the company could bypass the institutions in efficiently raising the requisite funding whenever needed, they would surely do that. For the investor on a net basis, their investment is worth more if their starting position is not reduced by fees, as the amounts they have invested are fully available for their intended purpose, that being for the company to pursue its stated objectives.

While distorted markets create short-term opportunities for one group over another, in a free-market economy, the key participants, the investors and the enterprises, should seek to always maximise the efficiency of the market for the long-term success of each. Theoretically, a system that fundamentally and relentlessly pursues the maximisation of willing and able supply and demand participants will optimise company values and, thus, funding outcomes.

While understanding that the utopian state of maximum efficiency and value optimisation may be beyond practical accomplishment, the participants can nonetheless aspire to go as close as possible to this end. Removing the systemic roadblocks through adopting new technologies and innovative ways of thinking could significantly free up the mechanisms of supply and demand to level, and open up the playing field to the maximum number of participants. Maximising the number of participants on the supply and demand sides is key to improving the optimal financing of enterprise and increasing the all-important choice in investment opportunities to as many investors as possible.

14. THE COST OF EXCLUSION: CAPITAL MARKETS AND THE DEMOCRATISATION OF INVESTMENT

What is the impact on capital markets of 'exclusivity'?

By definition, exclusivity excludes. In capital markets, exclusivity manifests in limiting the number of participants and restricting the supply and demand of funding and information. This ultimately curtails investment returns and human endeavours through the opportunity costs of the unrealised benefits that these two core market pillars could engender.

'Centralised regulation', which ideally should advocate inclusivity, has paradoxically become a structural contributor to this exclusivity. Historically, centralised regulation has been the most significant driver of investor protection. However, in recent years, attempts to achieve this protection have, ironically, bolstered investment exclusivity. To examine this provocative assertion, one may consider the following virtuous mantra for optimising supply and demand in capital markets that few would dismiss as an inappropriate aspiration:

Every investment dollar, every investment opportunity, available to everyone.

Yet, a discerning cynic might argue that the journey from 'principle to practice' in the current reality paints a different picture that could be summarised as:

Every investment dollar, every investment opportunity, tightly controlled and demarcated based on wealth, geography, education, regulatory frameworks and networking circles.

While societal structures defined by social classes in Anglo societies have generally dissipated over the last century, new forms of these demarcating structures have concurrently risen within capital markets. Opportunities and financial wealth are seemingly ring-fenced for the elite, to the exclusion of the lower demographic sectors of society.

Western democracies ardently uphold their concept of political democracy, but sightings of the everyday application of true democratic principles are more elusive. A universal contaminant to this applied democracy is the concept of 'exclusivity', which fundamentally contradicts the democratic ethos. Democracy, in its essence, grants everyone a voice. Extending the idealism of this principle, each individual's input should be able to be received, understood, contemplated, and integrated so that it proportionately influences the decision-making process.

Yet, in capital markets, various factors diminish the democratic ethos. These factors include wealth concentration, inherent human greed, layered regulations, time efficiency, and the natural human tendency towards minimal effort, resulting in unequal access to investment opportunities.

Well-meaning legislators and regulators try to protect smaller investors by requiring intermediary participants to follow an evolving body of procedures and protocols in presenting financial opportunities to their clients. However, the commercial result is that investors with smaller amounts of capital, while possibly having the risk reduced of receiving and acting on poor or fraudulent advice, end up receiving less advice. Or, worse still, no advice at all, as the compliance cost and effort for the intermediary service provider outweighs the potential benefit to the advisor or offeror in making the opportunities available to the investor.

Moreover, why would a corporate finance team make 100 calls to smaller investors to raise the requisite monies for specific investment opportunities when they could just make a few calls to the larger ones? The inequitable scenario ensues with those 'few' gaining the first, and often the only, access to what are retrospectively the 'best investment deals', and the remainder of the public investors only receiving exposure to the opportunities that 'the few' did not want.

Consider an individual with money to invest, who is looking to create an investment portfolio. Assume this individual lacks the knowledge and experience to make informed direct investment decisions. They may also not be familiar with the mechanisms of how they would find and negotiate an investment in any given company's shares and monitor their portfolio performance to optimise returns. This investor profile represents a significant proportion of the global population. The mechanisms to make genuinely informed investments are often obscured by the complexities of opaquely delivered information, blunt regulatory hurdles, systemic exclusivity that restricts access, and the cultural parochialism of capital markets, which is increasingly mismatched with global commerce.

Determining the investment worthiness of companies can be remarkably complex, despite the universality of critical elements underpinning any given opportunity's value.

Is the company profitable?
Will it be profitable in the future?
Is it growing?
Can it grow?
Is it funded?
Who is running it?
Etc.

These simple questions can be difficult to answer. As the most prescient ones are about the future, the answer will always have caveats. It is only the answers to those forward-looking questions that are practically relevant to the prospective investors, as they will only be exposed to the returns following their point of investment, not prior.

So, how can an investor identify potential investments, assess their value, make the investment, monitor performance, and ultimately realise a return?

The contemporary answer to this question is an increasingly complex web of intermediaries where even the financial advisors are detached from the end investments, as each intermediator—a fund, a fund of funds, an index fund—only holds relationships with their adjoining links in the long and twisted chain between the originator of the cash flows (the company) and the investor that seeks a return exposure.

From the investor's perspective, each intermediary in this labyrinthine system theoretically exists to provide advice or access through which the investor can achieve net returns by navigating processes and information that the investor otherwise could not, or does not want to, manage themselves. However, the intermediaries are parasitical as they do not generate returns from their activities, but instead draw on the investor's gross return or the company's gross funds to create and maintain the barrier that separates them. The two parties that lose out are the ones at either end of the line: the investor whose money it is, and the enterprise for which their investment is intended.

The losses incurred can be quantified for each in terms of both time and financial return. Survival is innate to all entities, both biological and corporate, and the more an entity establishes its identity in size and power, the more it galvanises its expectation of continuing to survive. The mechanisms become an industry unto themselves. A key underpinning element that sustains the investment industry is exclusivity. The exclusion of investors from investment opportunities, and consequently, on the company's side, the exclusion of investment. This exclusion is not usually directly intentional—it is primarily structural.

Segregation is not enshrined in the elemental underpinnings of capitalism or capital markets. Instead, it is the byproduct of the repeated practical application of capitalism by human beings inherently drawn to closed groups of preferential treatment. While such an approach may befit personal or family environments, in a capital markets system that champions free will and choice, the continued propagation of these silos is hypocritical to the spirit of capitalism and is a systemic flaw. Silos can manifest due to geographic borders, institutional structures, educational barriers, professional domains, and technology. New entities, both public and private, arise within these silos, determined to ensure their survival. Notable examples include investment banking, financial advice, and the regulatory bodies that uphold them. These siloed empires attract through manufactured dependency and simultaneously separate their core stakeholders—investors and companies—all while benefitting handsomely, and, it will be argued, unnecessarily, at the expense of both parties.

In the spirit of the 'free market', exclusivity should be identified and weeded out by market participants wherever it emerges. Everyone desires inclusion. Or, at the very least, the option to participate. A genuinely 'free market' can only flourish when the capitalist system prioritises the maximisation of inclusivity, leading to more investment funds and greater commercial creativity.

While this discourse might seem like mere idealist discontent without providing viable solutions, the decentralist movement and its associated technologies offer the will and the tools to foster a culture of inclusivity within capital markets. Each key societal stakeholder—the government, entrepreneurs, investors, and citizens—has a part to play in this reimagined approach, albeit in forms that may differ considerably from their historical roles.

PART V:

THE REVENUE REVOLUTION: DISRUPTING TRADITIONAL INVESTMENT DYNAMICS

"You're the voice, try and understand it..."

WHERE'S MY CAKE?

Imagine you own a sugar mill, and were asked to invest your sugar in a team determined to make a cake each month, of which they promise you a slice. "Oh great, I love cake!" you say. "Sure, I'll invest in that!"

Each month the team tries to make a cake, and eventually, it works out. However, at the end of each month, you turn up for your piece of cake, and you're told that there's none left as the team has eaten it all. Then they start making two cakes and three however, the team grows in size and appetite, and you keep turning up for your cake only to be told that, again, it's all been eaten. Then the cake-making team upscales and tells you how good the cakes are getting, and you think, surely now I'll get to taste some and low and behold, you turn up for your cake, and you're told that, while there is some left this month, the team says, "Oh, we're saving it as we might want to eat more than we produce next month."

Frustrated, you follow your investment of sugar by investing your time in understanding what the cake-making team are doing, and why there's never any cake left for you. You gather as much information as possible from the open-mouthed but tight-lipped team, and determine that the cake makers are not running as efficiently as you think they could be.

You start agitating the cake-making team, telling them they should eat less and make more. The management team don't like that, and the best team members start looking to join other cake-making teams and the quality and quantity of the cakes you're invested in start to diminish. You find yourself hungry and frustrated with the whole process and start questioning why you would bother investing in any further ventures.

You decide to try and sell your entitlement to the leftover cake, and prospective buyers, seeing there hasn't been any cake forthcoming to date, question the value of the asset you're selling. You can only revert to the so far unfulfilled promise of future cake. You're forced to concede that your cake investment is tangibly worthless.

Conversely, the flour mill owner comes across the same cake-making team and says I'll only invest if I get the first slice of each cake the team makes. The team accepts the offer and delivers the first slice of each cake fresh to the flour investor every month.

The flour investor enjoys their cake and wishes the team well in devouring as much of the remaining cake as they see fit, provided they keep delivering the entitled portions upfront, which the team is keen to do as they all love cake and the more they make, the more there is for everyone to enjoy.

Eventually, the flour mill owner is so full of cake that they decide to sell their interest. Cake-hungry investors seeing perfect record of regular cake deliveries, value the investment accordingly, and the satisfied cake-filled investor happily moves on to their next investment.

15. Understanding where Investors sit in the Conventional Cashflow Queue

Companies engaged in commerce generate revenue that results in gross cash inflows. As the cash comes in, it's spent on the items required to generate future cash inflows. Each expenditure line item deducts from the cash inflows and has a defined place in the order of expenditures from the first dollar spent to the last.

There are only a limited number of gateways for external funders to gain direct exposure to a company's future cash flows. Each gateway occupies a specific position in the 'cashflow queue', where recipients are queued based on the ordering of entitled portioning of gross topline inflows. The 'Cashflow Queue' is a critical concept to overlay on the various external funding strategies available. External financiers seek a tangible return on their committed funds, which may be achieved—to the extent their interest provides for it—by selling their entitlements to another party, or receiving a portion of the company's cash flows.

Deductions from gross cash inflows pertain to a company's obligation to suppliers, employees, shareholders, and taxation authorities. Irrespective of the contractual or legislative strength that a party may possess, it logically follows that those lower in the Cashflow Queue face higher return risk than those higher up. This is because recipients higher in the line may leave little or no remaining funds for those who follow.

In laying the foundation for the subsequent chapters, it is appropriate to summarily revisit a select few of the conventional equity and debt instruments, and their relation to the Cashflow Queue concept:

Equity

In the conventional sense, equity ownership is the ownership of a company's net cash flows. The value of this ownership for each respective holder is based on their percentage ownership. Unless transferred or leveraged, the manifestation of that financial value only occurs when the company distributes monetary amounts to the owners, typically as dividends. Two key caveats exist in this relationship: first, funds must be available after satisfying all operational and discretionary expenses, and second, those running the company elect to pay a dividend, which they are generally not strictly obliged to do, barring specific structured arrangements.

Investors naturally value 'yield' because it is the manifestation of fundamental value in corporate ownership. Yield is the income derived from a financial instrument without transference of ownership. Yield is tangible, and thus it is valued significantly higher than capital growth, which is only of notional significance unless acted upon by selling, resulting in the diminishment of ownership through the foregoing claim on future net cash flows.

Yield is a direct value transfer from the investment back to the investor. This derivation of tangible value from the outcomes of entrepreneurial activities embodies the essence of holding a percentage ownership in a company's net cash flows. Conversely, the value of 'capital growth', notwithstanding market-bestowed value, is fundamentally imaginary. Capital growth can only be realised if an available market exists to sell the instrument. The value of capital growth is connoted by speculation on the future realisation of net cash flows through prospective yield or sale.

If a person goes outside, sees clouds in the sky, puddles on the ground and puts their hand out and it gets wet, then it's raining—that is yield. On another day, if a person sees clouds in the sky and decides not to water their garden as they think it will rain tomorrow, that is speculating. Yield is worth something today, speculation is worth nothing today, other than that bestowed by one's imagination of the future. While there are many well-utilised formulas that attempt to make future value 'real' today, they really only serve to provide quantification to imagination, that then provides a basis for trading it.

Consider Company A, which is aiming to pay 5% per annum on the funds invested through dividends to the investor each year, and then Company B, which offers the prospect of a compounding 10% capital gain per annum though no dividends. Based on general average comparative market valuations of dividend to capital growth companies, all things being equal, investors in the main are likely to choose Company A. Not only is the value transfer tangible, but the realisation of that value does not entail a loss of ownership. The owner continues to hold the same percentage interest in the net cash flows following each yield payment.

A universal tenet of the human condition is that each person needs and values regular income, and they can either make it themselves or invest their money in others that provide it for them. The problem with valuing capital growth is that while holding, it amounts to only a 'paper profit'. It does not add any tangible beneficial value to the person's life. An uplift in one year may reverse the following year, resulting in zero net benefits on paper and zero real benefits across the two periods.

Yield is fundamentally a progressive realisation of value and perceptively a much safer option than betting on a future cash-out event to realise capital growth. The phrase 'Cash is King' is often quoted in the business world, and for the investor, 'cash now' is typically perceived as worth more than the prospect of 'cash later'. This concept is strikingly evident in average market valuations, particularly during periods of prevalent market uncertainty when 'future value' is markedly discounted. In buoyant markets, when the dichotomy of 'capital gain versus yield' loses relevance in capital markets, it signifies a move towards future volatility in equity pricing when the exuberance subsides. This shift arises as investors grapple with the fundamental concept underpinning the value of share ownership—namely, the tangible realisation of value from their proportional right to net cash flows.

While not the sole panacea to this source of market volatility, greater diversity in investment opportunities, that is, more supply, to meet investor demand should theoretically help to maintain a closer link to intrinsic value in market valuations. Of course, this would in turn depend on the demand element in the price interaction.

Debt

In contrast to equity holders, debt providers speculate less on the future value of net cashflows as their exposure ends with the repayment of borrowed funds and the fulfilment of associated contractual fees and interest payment obligations. Unlike the uncapped upside and downside interests of the subject company's shareholders, debt providers narrow their risk and return exposure by holding a higher position in the Cashflow Queue, typically extracting their return with more control and frequency.

Furthermore, the debt provider will generally seek to mitigate their downside risk by acquiring an optioned interest in the company's tangible assets, such as property or equipment. These assets hold a market value separate from the company's future cash flows. If the borrower defaults on the agreed repayment terms, the lender may exercise their option to force an asset sale to recover the outstanding amounts from the proceeds. However, this action is not the preferred course as it causes pain and precludes future lending prospects. In practice, the lender strives to ensure that their return is delivered by a sustainable business that will continue to borrow, thus being a future potential income source for the debt provider for as long as they maintain their custom.

Debt provision has evolved into various forms, and specific approaches aim to narrow the exposure from general speculation on the company's overall future performance to a more direct exposure to specific revenue line items. These strategies typically involve promoting the debtor to a higher position in the Cashflow Queue in exchange for relinquishing their general hold on the company's assets secured through blanket liens, in favour of strengthening it on select target company assets. One relevant example for future reference in the forthcoming chapters is Debtor Finance that targets specific revenue line items, and even drills down to individual customers of the company by implementing mechanisms to deduct owed monies as the company receipts its funds before other expense deductions. As will be explored, debtor financing is an instrument of traditional finance that, as an augmented concept, could be applied more broadly to company finance with the appropriate application of new technologies.

Traditional debt, which provides a more general exposure to cash flows, positions debt providers alongside other business expenses in the Cash Flow Queue. In contrast, debtor financiers sit ahead of general operating expenses in the Cashflow Queue, essentially at the front of the line, collecting their dues as the company receives its gross cash inflows.

The mechanisms to achieve this require scrutinising the company's paying clients. These clients, known as 'debtors' when owing the company for items they have purchased, are assessed for creditworthiness to determine if the financier will advance monies against the company's impending payments. Provided the debtors fulfil their invoice payments, the financier is repaid along with their interest and fees. The company benefits from a reduced working capital window through this pre-payment of invoices. The working capital window—the time period between operational cash expenditure and cash inflow—is a key determinant for growth. The shorter this period, the less cash must be preserved to fund the day-to-day operations, making more funds available for scaling operations to promote business growth and resultant stakeholder prosperity.

Debtor Finance, also known in other variations as 'Invoice Financing' or 'Factoring', is a traditional tool for financing businesses that either do not wish to, or cannot otherwise access alternative forms of debt finance and that cannot or otherwise do not want to, undertake new equity issues. The company also typically gains a narrowing of recourse exposure to the financier, which is expressly limited to the targeted assets—the debtor accounts.

The nature of debtor financing places significant control over the repayment of lent monies in the lender's hands and simplifies the creditworthiness proposition. The financier's primary concern is the individual debtors and the nature and sustainability of their arrangements with the company. The financier receives their payment as the business receives its income. This offers financiers a more finely tuned view of cashflows and assurance of receiving their owed amounts. However, it also creates a comparatively higher administrative burden, as they must stay closer to the business, ensuring contractual parameters are honored.

The critical contextual significance of this form of finance is that it includes an explicit third-party acknowledgement of the value of the gross revenue line, and an active engagement with it. The overall creditworthiness of the company, though secondary to their primary concern, remains crucially important. If the company cannot fund its operations from revenues net of the amounts paid to the funder, then the company will cease to operate. Consequently, the revenue line will end with it. However, the funder has a rolling exposure that seeks to synchronise with the company's working capital cycle, providing relative protection from significant losses.

Bonds

Another pertinent cashflow lending instrument to consider in the context of the Cashflow Queue, and one of the oldest forms of third-party funding, is the Bond.

A Bond is a debt security issued by an entity and purchased by investors. The Bond's backing is typically restricted to the issuing company's payment ability, which hinges on its future cash flows. Both governments and companies issue Bonds. As the term suggests, 'Corporate Bonds' are issued by companies and are essentially another form of debt financing. In traditional Bond markets, a prospective issuing company must demonstrate a consistent earnings profile to garner market appetite for their debt securities and provide a coupon rate (or "yield") that reflects the associated risk—the risk that the Company will have issues honouring their obligations. A company with a higher perceived credit quality may be able to issue debt at comparatively lower rates. On the other hand, if the collective market determines a company's outlook to be uncertain, it will need to offer a higher yield to stimulate market demand for its debt. At some point in the price curve, the yield percentage that the company would have to pay its prospective Bondholders becomes prohibitive, considering its working capital requirements. As such, the accounting rationale for seeking external funding in the first place becomes untenable.

In traditional capital markets, Corporate Bonds are a favoured funding source for larger companies, as evidenced by the fact that the Bond market in the United States is roughly double the size of the stock market. A key underlying reason for this is the lower perceived risk, both in terms of investment return and risk profile, compared to share ownership. Much like shares, the Bond price, in theory, is calculated with reference to the present discounted value of future cash flows. The primary distinction is that the Bond's value is centred on the cash flows associated with it, rather than the entire enterprise. The relationship of the value of the Bond to the issuing company's value is implicit, as the company must be capable of fulfilling the obligations of the Bond terms.

Bonds are typically fixed-income investments designed to generate steady income and safeguard the principal amount invested. When investors purchase a Corporate Bond, they lend money to the company. Conversely, when investors purchase shares, they acquire a percentage of the company's future net cash flows. The cash flows associated with Bond ownership are typically known, whereas the cash flows arising from shares are comparatively unknown.

If a company enters bankruptcy, its Bondholders and other creditors will be paid from any residual value before its shareholders. This is another element that theoretically suggests that Bonds are 'less risky' than shares. However, in practice, if the company collapses, the investors either lose their principal amount or incur the opportunity costs of having their capital tied up and unavailable for other investments until the external administration process concludes and their funds are released.

The transient nature of Bond financing can appeal to the company's existing shareholders as it offers funding without the undesirable strings attached to other forms, such as issuing new shares, which dilutes the future cashflow ownership and control of the existing shareholders.

One of the hurdles hindering the widespread adoption of Bonds is the pre-determined limited upside and the technically unmitigated downside, with yield –the upside– typically being the only lever to stimulate sufficient investor demand to compensate for the downside risk. With this proposition, investors are inclined towards safety to reduce the weighted probability of default to the point where the modest yield outweighs the risk. Consequently, only the largest and safest institutions in the world can offer this.

By their nature, Bonds usually attract yield-focused investors. Even though Bonds can be on-sold, the investor profile seeking meaningful exposure to capital gains as well as yield will likely overlook Bond markets favouring direct exposure to dividend-paying shares. However, earning a return through dividends carries significantly more risk than Bonds at the company level. Firstly, the investor must submit to the abilities of the company's management to generate revenue—gross cash inflow. Secondly, the management will spend less money to produce this revenue than it receives, ensuring the company makes a profit—net positive cash flow. Thirdly, the yield-seeking investor must then hope that the company's board and management will decide to distribute the post-tax operational surplus to shareholders rather than 'reinvest' the funds in the company's future cost structures.

Once every expenditure item—from the cost of goods sold, debt repayment, and employment costs through to non-cash items such as depreciation and impairment, and finally, tax payments and retained earnings-are deducted, dividends, if they are determined to be paid at all, occupy the very last position in the Cashflow Queue. Each dollar received in revenue makes a long, and a far from certain, journey through all the expenditure line items that seek to consume it before making it to the other side of 'net cash flows' before it can then be potentially available for dividend payments.

Yet, the investor's expectation of receiving these dividends underpins the intrinsic value of their investment. The structure of net cash flow distribution upon which conventional share ownership is founded necessitates an exceptional level of trust in the company's management to deliver a tangible return to shareholders. The theoretical and practical downside to dividend dependency is this agency risk, contributing to the unpredictability of dividends, the inconsistency of payments, the extensive research to determine future dividends, and the frustration experienced by investors when dealing with executives whose personal motivations are not aligned with the owner's in maximising dividend payments.

Relative to the dynamism of human imagination and enterprise, the traditional design of the core debt and equity instruments, which are meant to bring useful material things into being through funding commercial enterprise, is not fit-for-purpose. The entrepreneurial spirit that stirs capital markets naturally strives to create new products. However, without addressing the system's foundation, the new ways of offering money to fund enterprises and attract investors will only be based on the old ways.

Starting with the two core funding pillars of debt and equity that are directly tethered to the future cashflows of enterprise, an evolving web of derivative financial instruments has been allowed to flourish. For example, with one degree of separation from the share ownership of the company's cash flow, a Call Option gives its owner a right to buy the share at a specific price within a defined time period. The option itself has no value aside from that which it derives from the value of the underlying share. From the nucleus of value where the core asset—the cash flow—resides, there are expanding concentric circles of derivative products that are incrementally distanced from their ultimate underpinning fundamental value. As the derivates are layered down it becomes increasingly challenging for the investor to trace the fundamental value of their investment back to that original income-producing operational asset.

Each derivative has a unique risk and return profile that the humble share, limited by its defining characteristics, cannot offer. This limitation invites the invention of new derivative instruments. While creativity will always aspire to generate more, if a share, viewed as a financing instrument, was more flexible and dynamic, the investor could remain within that nucleus of value ascribed by the income generated from human endeavour—company cash inflows. This could occur while calibrating how the investor obtains their desired exposure to the asset through a direct relationship without the need to introduce derivative products.

Similarly, the company seeking investment could customise the instrument to suit its evolving financial requirements. A company's demand profile for external finance changes throughout its lifecycle, and the permanence and rigidity of traditional equity finance engender legacy arrangements that, all things being equal, persist with increased diminishment to the future net financial value and control of the founders as the company grows.

If a company could dynamically 'tune' its funding mechanisms to best suit its transient requirements and minimise the potential for future legacy issues, it would, subject to acceptable pricing, undoubtedly do so. Likewise, the investor could improve the calibration of their ownership exposure to the company's future cash flows to meet their specific requirements at a competitive expected return, relative to other offerings. This 'tuning' aims to generate a more precise resolution of the risk-return profile, enhancing the pricing outcome.

While numerous examples of individually tailored arrangements exist, such as royalty splits on intellectual property and other defined gross or net revenue streams, the supply and demand pools remain limited regarding a competitive and accessible public market. Limited participation curtails the opportunity to optimise each instrument's pricing point, leading to bubbles of market exclusivity that limit broader investor access to each unique transaction. It reinforces the prevailing argument herein that market exclusivity suppresses supply and demand and, sadly, produces sub-optimal outcomes for companies and investors alike.

With the technology now available for establishing global communities where no one is necessarily excluded, it opens the possibility for a standardised global capital markets platform to broaden opportunities for all participants. As postulated in the forthcoming chapters, such a platform could enable investors and enterprises to meet, negotiate, execute, facilitate, monitor, and finalise highly calibrated arrangements in a completely open-market environment.

16. A Paradigm Shift:
Reshaping the Agency-Owner Dynamics

The fundamental common ground between debt and equity providers resides in their shared pursuit of returns. As the principal generators of such returns, for-profit companies are obliged by their inherent nature to strive for profit from their undertakings.

The teams of people and resources required to run companies come at a cost, and that 'cost' is controlled by those same teams of people yet borne by the company's owners. These people are handing over their life energy, time, efforts, knowledge, and skillsets to operate the company on behalf of and for the benefit of the owners. They require equipment, offices, transport, utilities, insurance, professional service providers and other resources along the way to fulfil their great and, in a sense, notwithstanding their compensation, altruistic task as they toil for the benefit of the shareholders. In the event of the management team's success in generating sufficient revenue to cover all associated expenses, any surplus funds can be reserved for future costs or distributed amongst the company's owners as dividends.

The company's owners anticipate that the 'agency costs' are judiciously allocated and competitively priced. However, as noted, this system relies heavily on trust, as the agents effectively control the company's funds. Thus, the owners must hope that the agents operate prudently and economically, optimising the company's resources to maximise returns to the owners. The quantifiable magnitude of this return serves as the defining measure of asset value for the owners.

Value-seeking investors are constantly concerned about the expenditure items of the companies they invest in. 'Profitless volume', although possibly rewarding for the agents through their remuneration deducted from company expenditures, provides no value to the investor. The practical downside of reliance on dividends is apparent in the excessive investigation and research required to anticipate the agents' performance and the future financial outlook of the company.

Additionally, there is the challenge of dealing with management that has inherent personal motivational drivers in certain expenditure lines that may be at odds with maximising the owner's net cashflows. Prospective investors typically focus on the potential revenue a company could generate—"How big this thing could get!". They may be lured by the macro theme, sector, or outlook, amongst other factors, that suggest the company may thrive. However, without even considering the expenditure lines in detail, numerous risks are involved in backing management's ability to capitalise on the opportunities to generate revenues in any given pursuit.

Agents and investors are fundamentally aligned in their shared revenue generation goal, which forms the basis for all ensuing cashflows. However, within the framework of the Cashflow Queue, agents are paid according to their contractual rights, sourced from the expenditure lines. In contrast, investors are paid subsequently, as per their rights, at the distributed net profit line. This distribution largely depends on the agents' discretion in terms of both quantity and timing. This situation creates potential issues for investors, as due to the inherent stakeholder incentive structure, investors are significantly more personally concerned about the profit line than the agents.

What if, hypothetically, the owners were positioned ahead of the agent's direct interests in the Cashflow Queue?

This implies that they would receive their returns from top-line cashflows, preceding agency costs, rather than bottom-line post-agency costs.

What ramifications would this have for the owners and agents?

In such a scenario, the owners could concentrate on the company's ability to generate top-line revenue, reducing their concern about the agents' ability to optimise the profit line, as their relationship with net earnings would switch from direct to indirect. Although no longer the exclusive source of tangible value, the net cashflows would remain relevant to the extent that they sustain and enhance their top-line interests. This arrangement could afford the agents more freedom to genuinely manage the company 'as they see fit', a phrase frequently employed in corporate law. The agents could operate with less interference from external owners in their operational dealings and decisions regarding expenditure.

If you're not growing, you're shrinking.

In a competitive market, any company not seeking to acquire market share will likely be losing it to those that are. Typically, revenue optimisation is universally acknowledged as a rational and uncontested objective for all company stakeholders. While prudent reinvestment of net cash flows in the business and a consequent reduction or delay in dividend yield may sometimes be appropriate, maximising revenues is almost always a key objective.

Why not let investor risk primarily rest at the revenue level?

This approach allows the executives to deploy funds without enduring the stress of narrowly profit-focused investors being preoccupied with minimising every accounting item below the top line. The investors, in turn, obtain the returns they seek without troubling management over allocating the profit line between dividends and re-investment. Investing directly at the revenue line could significantly alleviate agency risk by aligning stakeholder interests and providing greater certainty for investors and simplicity for the company's management. There is more than enough agency risk for investors to be concerned about at the revenue line, below that, it's little wonder, for this reason alone, that most of the world's population to date has nothing to do with direct share ownership.

A shift in investor focus from bottom to top-line cash flows would imply that expenditure decisions on wages, marketing, administration and other overheads would no longer directly impact the investor's return. The impact would be indirect, to the extent that those factors affected the company's future revenues.

The 'profit motive' remains relevant but within a more appropriate context. The overriding determinant is that the company remains a going concern, capable of sustaining and growing the revenue line. The livelihood and reputation of the executives and the returns for investors depend on this, providing multiple motivations to ensure the company's profitability and self-sustainability. The key lies in aligning contribution and control within this restructured cash flow hierarchy.

For example, consider a company that sells shares representing 5% of its future revenues. If the company's revenue line was $1m per annum and investors paid a valuation of five times revenue—$5m—they would have invested $250,000 for their 5% ownership of revenues. If the revenue remains at $1m per annum, their yearly return is $50,000. However, the investors' annual return doubles if the business can use the invested funds to grow the revenue line to $2m. The profit line remains vital to the company's management and arguably becomes even more important to them as their effective percentage control of the revenue line diminishes. Profitability, however, depends entirely on revenues and the subsequent management of expenditures. Therefore, the business owner and the investors align in their desire to optimise the revenue line.

Top-line company investment, in contrast to the prevailing bottom-line approach, could offer a sense of liberation for investors and agents alike. This freedom would extend to internal stakeholders, such as management and directors, who could control cashflows without the obligation to external investors to maximise profitability. Additionally, investors could be freed from the layered ambiguity of profit-based returns and the mystery surrounding the fundamental valuation of their investment. Management would be free to create a lifestyle for themselves, provided it optimises the revenue line. If no profit is left, the sustainability of the living environment they have created is compromised, so the incentive to operate sustainably is paramount for management. It will also drive capital pricing at the revenue share level as investors naturally seek sustainable revenues.

Decoupling from the profit-obligation allows the agents—management—to adopt a philosophical mindset that may conflict with profit maximisation without compromising their integrity, ethics or relationship with investors. That mindset may include paying above-market remuneration or elevating social and environmental causes. Under a revenue-based approach to share ownership, external investors do not need to compel, nor is there any agent-to-owner obligation, to maximise profit but only optimise it as the agents see fit to achieve the more common stakeholder goal of long-term revenue maximisation.

17. REBUILDING FINANCIAL MARKETS: ONE BLOCK AT A TIME

Blockchain is a technology in search of a business model. Distributed Ledger innovations carry the keys to unlock the doors between investors and companies. The complexity of financial markets, having developed over centuries and accelerating exponentially in the current one, are cannibalising its core participants—entrepreneurs and individual investors—through the proliferation of intermediaries that stand between them.

Each generation has the autonomy to design financial tools to suit their era. However, history shows that upon encountering novel technical innovation, there's a pattern of participants simply transposing traditional methods into the new technology without a reflective pause to reset the structural approach— this happens later. In the last few decades, internet advertising has experienced a similar trajectory. Initially, information and advertising were arranged and delivered on websites mirroring traditional print media practices. However, as platforms evolved beyond simply 'accelerating the old world', pioneers harnessed commercial creativity, laying the groundwork for unprecedented innovations previously inconceivable, offering superior technical, operational, commercial, and utility outcomes.

Distributed Ledger technologies provide the most significant opportunity since the internet's advent to align businesses with investors for their mutual benefit. This alignment could eclipse the existing, centralised financial markets in the foreseeable future. The path to transmuting the many ambitious proclamations into practical tools for all to use is complex. The successful architects of commercial applications dispense with any notion of being obligated to replicate old-world practices, as that unimaginative approach would undermine the opportunity.

The global market of investors and companies appears to be ready, and the search is on, to find 'real value'. Not just speculative apparitions, such as most of the cryptocurrencies that have emerged to date, which, while experimentally interesting, are fundamentally unnecessary, and furthermore, unhelpful in attracting enduring mainstream support and adoption. As with any innovation that promises to be more than a gimmick, it must be tangibly useful. Speculative currencies are not practically useful to people other than for speculating, and even then, like all speculation, it is only useful for those that are on the right side of it. For every winner, there is a corresponding loser.

However, the strident naysayers of crypto assets would do well to reflect on the speculative nature of existing national fiat currencies that have long since decoupled from anything akin to real value. Notwithstanding the arbitrage-based industry of interest payments on cash, the 'value placeholder' that traditional national currencies have become reflects that it has no fundamental value, only a transacting value—as it doesn't produce anything.

Like the initial conception of precious metal-based paper currency, blockchain technology allows for the divisibility of assets, recording ownership, and transferring ownership in previously unachievable ways. This attribute opens the door to contemplating and revisiting how people transact, invest, and access finance. As revisited in the preceding chapters, shares represent the division of net profit, enabling the recording, administration and transfer of ownership. The processes through which investors buy shares, receive entitlements during share ownership, and then sell the shares are facilitated by various central bodies replicated across sovereign states. Blockchain technology enables these processes to occur via a single, secure, verifiable software protocol, potentially eliminating the need for centralised bodies.

Self-executing or 'smart contracts' underpin cryptocurrencies and can exist universally, independent of sovereign state facilitation. They are governed by their own programming rules, which are transparent for all to inspect and evaluate. Tokens, in essence, are serialised units symbolising asset ownership. Conventional shares can be likened to tokens, representing an entitlement to a set allocation of the company's future distributed net cash flows.

While tokenisation of traditional shares might offer significant benefits in decentralising capital markets, before jumping straight to 'old-world replication' in new-world technology, a lateral tweak opens the door for a novel and enhanced approach to corporate ownership, uniquely enabled by blockchain. With the arrival of this new technology, the tokenisation of profits—the traditional model of 'shares'—may be less suitable for the global community in contrast to the comprehensive tokenisation of revenue, now made possible. The tokenisation of revenue could mark the next significant advancement in financing and investment. If embraced, it has the potential to elevate average global living standards, and the individual's sense of self-worth, through consequent positive behavioural impacts.

The historical antecedents to 'Revenue Tokens' are the debt instruments of Bonds and debtor finance facilities, which fundamentally involve revenue-based financing. Revenue Tokens introduce the potential to blend the top-line approach of these instruments with the benefits—and without the numerous drawbacks—of traditional bottom-line equity ownership. This allows for a finely calibrated shaping of the risk-return profile for any given exposure to the target investee company's future cashflows and, thus, a greater resolution on market pricing.

There have been various yield-level attempts in the rapidly emerging sector of decentralised finance, but they have yet to reach a universal standard with open mainstream acceptance and access. The opportunity here is not just to standardise but to productise tokenised revenue. This would directly pair companies and investors through a decentralised platform operated and controlled by the users: a decentralised community of investors and companies. Encapsulated in customisable Revenue Tokens, gross cashflows could become a tradable asset that optimises funding and investment.

Consider, for instance, a company deciding the proportion of its revenue line to be tokenised and offered to investors. The company is then responsible for adequately detailing its revenue line to investors, enabling them to develop an informed perspective on the acceptable yield as a percentage of the token's price, given the risk proposition at each point in time within a global investment opportunity marketplace. Companies could create and issue Revenue Tokens to raise capital from the global investor market.

In the traditional approach of investing at the bottom line, there is an implicit belief that a given company can generate revenues. Yet, investors depend on dividends for their returns, which are not always correlated to revenue growth. Revenue Tokens explicitly align the financial instrument with the investor's focus, and provide a more direct connection between actual and perceived value.

Many companies generate revenue for years before paying dividends. Investing directly at the revenue line significantly reduces the agency risk and provides greater certainty for the investor and simplicity for the company. The agents can then explicitly and genuinely communicate their merits to the investor, and associated stakeholder groups on multiple fronts, some of which may not be related to the pursuit of profit maximisation. Importantly, the agents can do this without compromising their financial obligations to the company's owners, provided that the revenue line is optimised. The alignment is likely to be much greater between the disparate stakeholders at the revenue line than at the profit line, as the former has a broader recipient base.

Theoretically, all companies, from the smallest proprietors to the largest multinationals and governments, could issue Revenue Tokens. Revenue Tokens could replace most existing financial instruments, even fiat currencies in the form of tokenised taxation income, as they can be configured by the issuer around the cash flow to function in the conventional sense as debt, equity, or a hybrid. Rather than creating layers of derivative instruments that progressively distance the investor from the source of cash flow, the same instrument could be applied with varying configurations keeping the relationship between the investor and their target cash flow as close as possible. Large and diverse organisations may issue Revenue Tokens for a specific subset of their business revenues, such as a regional hub, a particular project or product, or a licence royalty stream.

This allows for more flexibility to finely calibrate funding requirements and the pricing of that funding. In some cases, investors may be more inclined to invest if they do not wish to have an exposure to the entire business but are drawn to a specific part of that business, such as a division, an intellectual property asset, special projects, or specific geographic regions. Revenue Tokens provide a standardised means to narrow investment exposure to a particular revenue generator within a conglomerate. The critical common thread is 'tangible value'. Each revenue-based security, under the umbrella term of 'Revenue Token', derives its fundamental value from its attributed gross cashflows.

Once the issuing platform is established, the structures are only limited by cashflow sources, investor demand and imagination. By making the platform universally accessible to all enterprises and investors, the opportunity is open to everyone to participate to their desired extent.

18. Revenue Tokens: The Value Dawn of Decentralised Finance

Following from the previous chapter, Revenue Tokens present an innovative avenue for investment whereby investors engage at the top line of a company's income statement by capitalising on tokenised revenues and receiving a predetermined percentage or amount of gross revenue. Such tokens serve as a new financial instrument that can be issued through a decentralised platform by any entity inclined to offer them. Investors, in turn, are granted the liberty to evaluate these offers and determine their interest in investing. Consistent with the ethos of decentralisation, it's anticipated that Revenue Tokens will be traded on decentralised exchanges and that these tokens, while held, will generate income for the token holder, provided that the token issuer is generating revenue.

Companies that allocate a fraction of their revenue line for tokenisation issue a specific number of tokens. Each token represents a percentage claim on the company's gross revenues. When the company receives payment from its activities, token holders are paid their respective percentages, with the remainder of the revenue retained by the company. In essence, companies are selling a portion of their revenue in exchange for immediate liquidity and investing this cash to drive more substantial future revenues than would otherwise be possible. Companies could realise value from their future cash flows without diluting their direct ownership of net cash flows and, notably, without relinquishing ownership control subject to the terms of the Revenue Token.

Since every company and lifecycle stage is unique, Revenue Tokens can be 'tuned' to suit a company's specific needs, provided the resultant offering attracts the requisite investor demand. For instance, a company may allocate a fixed amount of its revenue, or a variable amount up to a predetermined cap, instead of a straight percentage. Once purchased, the tokens grant the holder a share of the company's revenues. These tokens, complete with their programmed entitlements, can then be resold on decentralised exchanges. Companies set the yield payment frequency corresponding to the token and can also apply additional parameters. This may include setting a minimum holding period before revenues are paid to the token holder, or implementing trading windows during which the transfer of ownership is suspended around sensitive events, such as yield payments or the announcement of financial results. The programmed settings of each token are transparent and open for the investor market to examine, evaluate, critique, and bid on.

Strategically designed, Revenue Tokens can offer the token holder rights to their allocated share of revenues according to the specific token's terms and nothing more, which stands in contrast to the comparatively broad and invasive entitlements attached to conventional shares. Unless especially provisioned, token holders do not have voting rights attached. 'Voting' with Revenue Tokens is affected exclusively 'by foot': Assuming a highly liquid global investor market is established, willing holders will buy or retain their tokens, and sellers will move on at their discretion. Consequently, companies will experience the investors' perspectives more acutely, as reflected in the funding cost. Consequently, 'popular' companies will be able to secure cheaper financing than 'unpopular' ones.

What constitutes a 'popular' company, as measured by its market value?

Ultimately, investors will determine this based on the valuations they are prepared to bid. While future revenue forecasts will be central to the investor's focus, profit projections will remain necessary however will likely become more peripheral in the investor's priorities, thus freeing management teams to genuinely embody ethical and altruistic positions in their expenditures. This approach contributes to building a more holistic representation of what a given company represents, or the type of 'corporate citizen' it aims to be without compromising its integrity as an optimised producer of returns for its investors.

Under a revenue-centric approach to finance and investment, broader societal benefits pursued by management that might adversely impact profit would no longer be of primary fiscal concern to external investors, provided the common objective of top-line revenues is pursued. Every worthwhile company should seek to achieve its vision and mission, a key measure of which is optimising revenues as it gives it a greater capacity to fulfil them. Companies will be free to dictate the commercial terms under which Revenue Tokens are offered. One possible mechanism might involve a set of 'dials' that company controllers adjust to establish what they believe is best for their business outlook, paired with considering a market competitive investment proposition to ensure the company receives the funding it seeks.

To illustrate the practical application of Revenue Tokens, the basic approach to the issue process might follow these steps:

1. Yield amount – the company might select either a or c, or b and c:
    a. A fixed sum in dollars
    b. A maximum amount
    c. A percentage of revenue
2. Yield frequency – yield payment frequency could be set at:
    a. Weekly, monthly, quarterly, or yearly, or
    b. No set frequency – for instance, it could be 'as received' or 'when received' for a pre-revenue company, or
    c. Nil yield – as may be the case for a token that pays out a specific amount at a certain date through the compulsory buy-back of the token as per 4.a. below.
3. If applicable, the issuing company may establish a minimum hold period before revenue is paid to token holders. Revenues will accrue to the tokens, but will be released once the tokens have been held by a holder for the stipulated minimum period. Tokens may be traded during this period,

with the revenues accumulating and paid to the first token holder who holds the token for the minimum period. In such instances, frequent trading within minimum hold periods can have a cumulative effect on the yield value of tokens experienced by the holder.

4. Buy-back price:

    a. A set buy-back price on a specified date, regardless of the market price

    b. A set buy-back price with no date

    c. No buy-back, although the company is free to buy back on the market in line with any other investor.

Within these general considerations, many derivative instruments currently utilised in capital markets may be accommodated through the issue of suitably customised Revenue Tokens. Each company would be free to assess its circumstances and adjust the Revenue Token settings to meet its specific requirements. The investor market can then bid, buy, and sell. Importantly, unlike most financial instruments currently available to companies and investors, Revenue Tokens are directly linked to the essence of business value—cash flows.

19. Revenue Tokens: The Confluence of Risk, Return, and Financing

Investment pricing is the driving determinant component of the financial world. In addition to market access—which, as covered earlier through enabling participation, determines the economic element of 'supply'—pricing is also underpinned and assigned by the intricate processes deployed in risk determination.

The returns on traditional bank term deposits often fail to simply keep pace with the compounding price growth expressed as inflation. Consequently, traditional cash investment instruments are often critiqued for "going backwards in real terms" based on the inflationary assumption in the comparative current and future 'spending power'. Notwithstanding this, investors typically, at least perceptively, find reassurance in investment instruments such as top-rated government bonds or term deposits, in which their principal remains safeguarded. Many investors are willing to forgo potential profits, or even tolerate marginal losses, as seen in the last decade in some government bonds, depending on central bank interest rate settings.

The staggering trillions of dollars stagnating in perceived low-risk investment instruments such as government bonds or term deposits signify investors' acceptance of a 'no risk, no return' proposition. A return without an inherent risk is an elusive concept. While it is broadly accepted that the pricing of returns and risk are correlated, the calibration of this correlation is fundamentally dependent on informed supply and demand channels. This supply and demand for capital, referred to collectively in the corporate sector as 'the market', are pivotal elements in the investment landscape.

Within this context, the Revenue Token enters the scene. Like its traditional counterparts, this new financial instrument is governed by market dynamics, dictating its key commercial aspects. A central financial driver in the price setting of Revenue Tokens is the yield, denoted as a percentage of the market price. For instance, a token priced at $1.00 with a 5% yield is expected to pay out $0.05 annually to its holder.

Theoretically, the larger the risk perceived in a Revenue Token, the more significant the return demanded to offset that risk. The potential downfalls include default on yield payments by the issuing company, thus interrupting the cash flow for the holder, or, in a worst-case scenario, the company running out of funds and folding, rendering the tokens valueless.

This approach to risk and return correlation is not novel. However, the Revenue Token brings a new level of adaptability in finely calibrating a risk and return profile to meet a company's financing needs. Conventional financial instruments have some flexibility, but their inherent structural customisation remains practically constrained without introducing yet another derivative instrument and, with it, a further separation from fundamental value.

With Revenue Tokens, companies can exercise financial control and make strategic decisions to buy back their issued tokens, either on-market or by exercising the rights programmed into the Revenue Token, to 'burn' them at any given time. 'Burning' a Revenue Token causes the revenue allocated to the tokens to revert to the company, flowing through its expenditure items and eventually contributing to the bottom line of net profit after tax. This mechanism should, in theory, have the effect of setting a natural market floor on the price of the Revenue Token, as while ever there is actual revenue being physically distributed to the token holders, there is an ongoing minimum incentive for companies to buy back their Revenue Tokens whenever the market price falls below the point, at which the company believes that the internal value of the revenue is greater than the market value.

In addition, the Revenue Token introduces a new variable input to the traditional costing model within the context of the weighted average cost of capital (WACC). The WACC is an academic concept that theoretically supports companies in deciding between debt or equity financing, helping them ascertain the most cost-effective means of funding. It aids in making the fundamental funding decision: "Is it less expensive to raise funds via the issue of new shares and dilute existing shareholders than it is to secure and service additional debt?"

Like its traditional counterparts, the retrospective vindication of whether to choose debt or equity financing significantly depends on the future share price. Suppose a company raises funds at a $1 per share and the following month the company's price has rocketed to $2. Excluding the incremental value of deploying the proceeds of the capital raise, in rough terms existing shareholders have essentially paid two dollars for each dollar raised. This suggests that debt financing would have been more cost-effective even at reasonably high market rates. Conversely, if the share price declines and remains low, equity financing retrospectively appears more attractive. This of course presumes that companies can access debt financing. If they cannot, the traditional financing equation becomes rather one-sided, revolving solely around when to raise capital based on the available issue price and the issuing company's prediction of the future share price.

This is where the concept of Revenue Tokens enters the fray, offering companies an additional option to assess the cost of forgoing gross cash flow ownership via a funding instrument that can adapt to future fluctuations in market valuation. If a certain Company A's market value is ten times its net profit, then, very simplistically and all things being equal, every additional $1 of profit would allow Company A to raise an additional $10 by the issue of new shares. In the context of Revenue Tokens, assuming a net profit margin of 10% for Company A, there is $10 of revenue for each dollar of profit. If the market values Company A at a revenue multiple of one, then traditional shareholders and Revenue Token holders would be entitled to the equivalent cash flow for the same investment made at this juncture.

The trade-off at the company level is that issuing either traditional shares or Revenue Tokens relinquishes a portion of entitlement to either net or gross cashflow to those investors in exchange for new funding. The company must then contemplate whether the returns from deploying the external funding will profitably offset the diversion of its cash flows. The company will naturally weigh the anticipated impact on cash flows as a percentage of the monies raised from a Revenue Token against a traditional share issue.

As noted in the previous chapter, the price of each Revenue Token should be expressed relative to its current yield. At the point of issue, the issuer explicitly sets the yield. For instance, a company may allocate 5% of its revenue to a Revenue Token Issue. If the issuer's total revenues amount to $10m per annum, then $500,000 of that gross revenue is allotted to the Revenue Token holders. If 10m tokens are issued at $1 each, the yield on each token is 5% based on that revenue. If the company's revenues subsequently increase to $20m per annum and the market price of the issued token remains steady at $1, the yield per token consequently moves up to 10%.

In practice, driven by the forces of supply and demand, if the given risk/return profile is unchanged, the yield relative to price should theoretically remain the same, prompting the token's market price to double to $2. However, the market's collective opinion on risk/return is ever-changing. Given that the company doubled its revenue, the market's view of the issuing company may improve, and the acceptable yield for new investors may reduce to 2.5%. Consequently, the market price of the issued tokens would rise to $4. If that occurs, the original investors in the token issue then see a 400% capital gain and a 10% per annum yield on their initial investment while they continue to hold.

The Revenue Token market allows active participation from both investors and issuing companies. As part of their financial control duties, issuers may buy and sell their tokens on the open market and issue new tokens as they deem fit. The issuer from the example above may raise additional funds by issuing tokens at a 2.5% yield, optimising their 'revenue-line asset' to capitalise on the favourable price movement.

The adoption of Revenue Tokens introduces a new dynamic that aims to effectively match and benefit those naturally invested at each level in the Cashflow Queue. This new financial instrument, which can sit alongside traditional profit-based share ownership, allows investors and issuers to position themselves wherever they feel most aligned with their interests.

Even pre-revenue companies, such as early-stage, mineral explorers, or research and development-focused firms, are not excluded from offering Revenue Tokens, just as they are not barred from traditional equity raising. When revenue is a distant possibility, it's safe to say that profit is even further off. Like traditional shares at the net cashflow level, a Revenue Token represents an entitlement to future gross cash flows, with the price set by buyers and sellers based on the collectively perceived risk/return profile. Revenue arrives well before any subsequent profit emerges after successive periods of positive earnings have worked through the offsetting accumulated losses.

For other companies that do not produce sufficient operating revenues to sustain external dispersal, they may still offer Revenue Tokens on the basis that one day the business will grow to a sufficient scale to make payments to the Revenue Token holders. This is akin to companies that reinvest profits rather than pay dividends, with a critical investor-centric difference. When designing its Revenue Token, an issuer could suspend the otherwise entitled cashflows to Revenue Token holders for an initial period, allowing those funds to be reinvested for business growth. In scenarios where purchasing a Revenue Token does not result in immediate yield payments, as with traditional share markets, the forces of supply and demand will determine the pricing appetite for the offer, taking into account the heightened risks associated with the delayed returns.

Delving into the potential administrative side of managing cashflows within the context of Revenue Tokens, consider the following illustrative examples:

Example A for a small company (S Company):

1. S Company has assigned 10% of all revenues to Revenue Tokens.
2. S Company logs its invoices on-chain.
3. The Revenue Token (RT) registers a programmed claim on 10% of the cash receipts resulting from invoice payments.
4. Payments of cleared funds enter the bank account; at this point, the RT reconciles with the 10% claim on the invoices and directs 10% to the company's RT trust account, denominated in digital currency.
5. The RT platform transfers digital currency from S Company's trust account digital wallet to the RT

holders in accordance with the terms of the RT.

Example B for a larger company (L Company) with multiple operating subsidiaries:

1. L Company has allocated a specific dollar amount each quarter to its issued RTs.

2. L Company maintains a float in its digital wallet to cover the periodic yield payments to the RT holders.

3. The RT platform distributes the yield payments to the RT holders in accordance with the terms of L Company's RT.

Example C for L Company:

1. L Company offers a non-yielding RT that comprises a one-off payment of $1 to repurchase the RT within twelve months from the issue.

2. L Company can set a fixed buy price or allow the market to bid up from a reserve price.

3. At the end of the twelve months, the RT platform distributes the amounts from L Company's digital wallet to each RT holder and burns the RTs.

L Company might also use the method described in Example A for a subsidiary or a special-purpose vehicle for a specific project. The flexibility of Revenue Tokens allows for a myriad of terms to meet the ever-changing funding requirements of the issuer over time.

There is potential universality in the Revenue Token (RT) platform, in that it could be designed to be accessible to every type of trading entity, from fledgling start-ups to multinational corporations, sports clubs to global associations, and even regional to national governments. The terms of the RTs offered will inevitably vary, reflecting the necessary balance between investor risk and return that also satisfies the issuer's financing requirements. For example, a start-up may need to allocate a larger percentage of its revenue—potentially uncapped or subject to a generous cap—to incentivise investors to take on the inherent risk.

Akin to government bonds, a sovereign government could allocate a fixed buy-back amount at a future point and allow the market to determine the price it is willing to pay for the perceived low-risk opportunity. Depending on market conditions, the price may only be a few percentage points less than the fixed buy-back price for a top-rated sovereign. It is important to note here that investment ratings play a crucial role in this hypothetical funding model, a topic to be expanded upon in subsequent chapters.

In the event of a company sale, unless the terms of the RT specify otherwise (such as a predetermined buy-back upon change of ownership), the RT obligations would be transferred to the new owner. Subject to the applicable local corporations legislation, if a company becomes insolvent, the RT would assume a creditor position, ranking alongside other unsecured creditors. However, in its design, a given RT may include certain safeguards, such as a minimum trust account float, to provide some risk-offset that would be factored in the market pricing.

These examples illustrate that the Revenue Token platform could operate as a fundamental tool, allowing users to create their customised version of the same financial instrument and letting the market establish the optimal price within their acceptable parameters. Like existing markets, the platform does not compel the issuer to accept a price outside these parameters. It is always open to issuers to withdraw their offer rather than proceed with the issue.

Naturally, introducing any new funding concept begs the question of 'governance.' Without effective governance, any initial excitement quickly wanes when tested in the field. For a system to be sustainable, it requires order and, importantly, efficiency within that order to ensure that the requisite administration processes do not overshadow the potential benefits.

PART VI

RETHINKING REGULATION: THE COLLECTIVE CONSCIENCE

"Make a noise and make it clear...

The King and the Mice

Once upon a time, a King saw that his village was being overrun by mice seeking to eat his cheese stores. Thinking about what may scare the mice away, he invited a family of cats to come in to deal with the mice.

The cats set upon and disarrayed the mice, and soon the King's cheese was safe. The cats enjoyed the sport of chasing the mice, and when they had done their job, they looked around for their next meal and discovered the fish in the King's larder. Displeased, the King welcomed a pack of dogs to come in and chase the cats away. The dogs then turned their attention to the King's flock of sheep, and on seeing this, the King sent for the lions. The dogs fled, as did every other animal in his fields.

The King, seeing his livestock devastated, considered the most giant herbivores around that would scare off the lions and leave his remaining animals in peace. Once invited, the elephant herd stampeded in, scaring away the lions but making it difficult for life in the village, as everyone feared being stomped on. The King's paddocks were trampled, and the elephants digested his vegetable gardens, leaving little food for his remaining livestock and the villagers.

Desperate to feed his village and retain his throne, the King knew he needed a new approach as the elephants were dominating, safe in the knowledge there were none bigger to come. However, fear did come for them, as the now wiser King did a deal with the mice allowing them to reenter the village and make their own cheese. The herd of elephants were overrun and disconcerted by the number, speed and agility of the mice. Their lumbering size was now a liability, as they had no way of countering or influencing the rapidity of their movement. Unneeded and unwanted, the elephants decided to abandon the village. The mice no longer threatened the King's larder, as they could feed themselves, and thus harmony was restored.

20. Rewriting the Rules: Regulation Fit for the Future

Progress is best preceded by reflection, and the mismatch of centralised and inherently parochial regulation with decentralising globalised markets has become abundantly clear. The pace of change in an increasingly digital world is accelerating through the exponential growth in the quantum and accessibility of information, analytics, and transacting, which is precipitating a correlated increase in the number of new entrants to global commerce. The challenges for border-confined regulatory institutions are consequently growing, as they attempt to maintain meaningful purviews over the market's latest creations and operations across novel enterprise approaches, assets and transaction mediums.

The time lags inherent in regulatory development mean that effective controls are often not in place when the damage is being done by the oblivious, or the malicious, actors that arrive at the frontiers of the latest market theme. In being so late to the event, the incoming regulatory framework, when finally enacted, often misses its intended culprits that have long since moved on to the next market innovation, and only serves to diminish the access of well-intentioned and innocent mainstream investors.

Regulation, however, is of paramount importance. To be genuinely efficacious, it must be contemporary, precisely targeted, and yield a net benefit for those participants who adhere to ethical principles. These attributes allow legislative and regulatory endeavours to fulfil their intended role of fostering an environment of trust and confidence, thereby encouraging widespread participation, which is an essential component for perpetuating any form of human interaction.

Moreover, as 'the economy' operates globally, capital, particularly in digital mediums of exchange that have been freed from the tether of state-issued currency, now features seamless portability. This advance helps to facilitate 'regulatory choice', wherein entrepreneurs can select the national regulatory framework they perceive as most favourable for their operations. However, when malicious people exploit this freedom, some investors may bear direct consequences, and all participants suffer indirectly as faith in the underlying structure is compromised by the corrupt actions of the few.

The combination of the comparatively thin resources directed towards regulatory processes in the sphere of global commercial engagement, the multi-layered legislative structures and procedures that new rules must navigate to become enacted, and the geographical boundaries of jurisdiction and enforcement that digital commerce readily bypasses are likely to persist in delivering less-than-optimal regulatory outcomes. The success of regulatory outcomes should ultimately be measured by the extent to which they stimulate enterprise and protect well-meaning stakeholders in the global economy.

For enduring success and to maximise participation, potential participants must clearly understand, and be confident in, the 'rules of engagement'. While the forerunning unscrupulous actors in a new and unregulated market may quickly amass significant financial wealth at the expense of others, their 'success' is a systemic weakness that manifests in a consequent and unproductive 'anti-development stage' characterised by newcomer deterrence resulting from the fear exploitation. Following that, regulatory bodies eventually cotton on and seek to unravel the corrupted playing fields. However, with their blunt application, such regulatory forays tend to also impede the interests and prospects of legitimate participants, further slowing the progress of the new system.

Many have looked towards the emerging frontier of the digital ledger in the search for innovative solutions. Yet, blockchain technology, while potent, has its limitations. For data to be integrated into the chain, someone must place it there. Many of the world's companies are private, and the details of their income, expenditure, and associated operations remain inaccessible to public scrutiny. In envisaging the possibility of blockchain technologies paving the way for a novel corporate regulatory framework, several foundational questions require consideration, including:

Why would proprietors of private companies voluntarily submit themselves to public scrutiny?

How can investors trust the companies they've invested in to willingly and consistently disclose the details of their operations that pertain to the value of their issued capital?

Given that legal proceedings and penalties are subject to local legislation and enforcement, is it feasible to conceive a global regulatory environment that inspires confidence among international participants?

Alignment is the lynchpin here, as the incentives mould the outcomes. Rules merely serve to discourage detrimental conduct. Rules are patches that seek to cover the structural misalignments in the system that open the prospect of desirable outcomes from negative exploitative behaviour. Nevertheless, at a particular juncture in the systemic continuum, the burgeoning layers of rules within the misaligned system become the system itself. As a result, the positive activities that the rules were designed to safeguard begin to languish under excessive, non-productive and costly administrative burdens of simply complying with the system, which becomes a systemic barrier in itself, leading to diminished participation and thus suboptimal market outcomes.

One of the most formidable tasks is attempting to supplant an existing, albeit suboptimal, structure with a new one. Rather than confronting the challenge directly, an alternative approach is to construct and present the new structure alongside the existing one, thereby providing a contrast and a choice for market participants rather than actively promoting disruption and attracting unnecessary confrontations with the unsettled incumbency.

The efficacy of punitive measures exerted by sovereign entities is waning in global capital markets as geographical borders grow increasingly less relevant with the digitalisation of commerce. Likewise, the associated authoritative bodies, bound by geography, are also becoming less relevant. Regulation must be dynamic and adaptive, moving in sync with the decision-making processes that was is designed to oversee. A global economy regulated solely by disparate sovereign states cannot be expected to deliver a seamless regulatory system for digital cross-border markets capable of instilling the degree of trust necessary to maintain broad market confidence and thereby maximise participation. International agreements between sovereign states aspiring to achieve a degree of uniformity are beneficial but are merely temporary 'patches'. Not all sovereign states will fall in with such agreements; moreover, the practical level of enforcement remains tethered to each state.

Confidence and participation are intrinsically linked. Although the incentives of value and convenience may be recognised, potential participants need to perceive a level of integrity in the system that reassures them that it will operate as expected—*"no surprises please!"* cry the participants that are trying to make forward plans.

As the imposition of new regulatory measures is typically reactive, the criminals exploit the new system with impunity and the subsequent mainstream fringe is burnt. Consequently, the new way of doing things is tarnished, compromising the system's integrity, and following a process of awareness, identification, and investigation, legislators and regulators devise a corrective response in the form of punitive penalties augmented by preventative measures requiring enhanced disclosure. Regulation, by its very nature, is a blunt instrument as it applies to all participants under the jurisdiction of the relevant authority. Often, an originating event may be committed by a minority subset of participants, triggering a regulatory response against this group that chooses to cluster around the lowest tier of market integrity. Subsequently, the entire market must adhere to regulations designed to curb the malign behaviour of the few.

Complying with regulation takes time, money, and effort, which are the same ingredients that go into the positive, productive behaviours that are aligned with the system and the interests of its participants. The result is that compliance displaces productivity such that in seeking to protect participants from the risk that they may encounter 'the few' parties that act against their interests, all participants must experience the detrimental effects of lower productivity caused by the diversion of resources away from serving their upside interests; their actual reason-for-being. Moreover, the rising cost of compliance must be balanced by an enhanced value extracted from the remaining resources applied to positive, productive activities. For the market participants tasked with compliance, the marginal cost of managing stakeholder requirements escalates over time due to the incremental nature of regulations.

At the company level, optimum productivity is achieved by a commercial approach that maximises results with minimal effort. Intermediaries in financial markets often generate income by charging a percentage of the financial value of their facilitated activities. This can be an explicit percentage, or an implicit tether based on charging a certain amount that, while not expressed as a percentage, by design, limits the potential custom to their desired target market. Generally, the larger the participant's assets, the larger the scale of their activities and the more value is derived for the intermediaries in applying their percentage.

For each intermediary, the value threshold for customer engagement rises, thus excluding an increasing proportion of the population from opportunities.

These opportunities may hold the potential for lucrative investment returns yet are inaccessible to most investors. While issuers may not require a wider audience to raise funds, they will never know if their transactions were optimally priced, as the limited participant numbers curtailed the price-setting efficiency of the supply-demand dynamics. While the increasing layers of rules and regulations serve their purpose in ensuring the system functions, there comes a point where the system is more preoccupied with supporting its frameworks of controls than serving its original purpose. At some point in this upward spiral, it is not new rules and regulations that are needed, it is a new system. One that can bring things back to earth.

In evaluating the merits of any enduring systemic approach, it could be helpful to reflect upon the question:

At what point are the participants serving the paradigm rather than being served by it?

Nature, particularly human nature, abhors a vacuum. Like any paradigm in applied philosophy, the incumbent model remains in place well beyond its logical expiry date until it eventually capitulates under the combined weight of its own limitations and an overwhelmingly superior alternative. Absent a new paradigm, the old one is likely to endure indefinitely. Capitulation causes pain and anguish, and presenting an alternate option that slowly gathers support from participants steadily making the switch provides a softer transition than a calamitous end and rebuild scenario.

Traditional corporate regulators may insist that regulations exist to safeguard participants. While this may be theoretically correct, there are two key practical challenges in optimising the realisation of this objective. Firstly, new capital market regulations tend to be retrospective. Following the establishment of a basic set of engagement rules that define and support a functioning market, subsequent additions and amendments are primarily reactionary, spawned by the actions of wrongdoers. New regulatory addendums are necessitated only when the core systemic participant safeguards prove to be inadequate. Secondly, commercial entities aim for efficient compliance. When resources that could otherwise be productive are deployed towards regulatory compliance, the subjected companies that only perceive a net cost are incentivised to minimise resources expended in meeting compliance obligations.

Notwithstanding the trending virtue signaling of entities that wish to be seen as upstanding corporate citizens against the backdrop of contemporary social issues, any expenditure of resources on non-productive purposes beyond the minimum required for regulatory compliance is at the expense of deploying those resources to profit-orientated activities to which the conventional company is obligated to pursue. Maximising the productive activities is where value is created for shareholders and thus is the overriding obligation of management. While there may be legitimate indirect arguments about its impact on company value, the systemic dichotomy remains such that the direct financial incentive to take all possible steps to maximise the spirit of compliance is simply not there in any legitimate direct sense against the backdrop of profit-obligation.

The consequence is that people do what they must do and no more. What they 'must do' is devote the necessary resources to complying with rules and regulations that were retrospectively designed to curb immoral behaviours that most people had no intention of ever doing anyway. Explicit rules and regulations are intrinsically centralised creations. Intrinsic, as they are typically the follow-on product of legislation enacted by sovereign states. Enforcement of this legislation falls to the centralised bodies created to administer the legislation via the regulatory framework. Centralised bodies still retain control even when various nation-states collaborate to develop codes of practice with cross-border reach.

As capital markets decentralise, how can centralised regulators possibly keep in step?

Government and commercial institutions will likely strive to retrofit centralised approaches onto decentralised technologies, though this is a misaligned grasp for continued relevance. Regulatory hard stops require system-driven disincentives, which naturally deter potential wrongdoers. However, to be effective and sustainable, decentralised participation requires decentralised moderating. In contrast to conventional regulators, programmed moderators operate within a system that offers financial incentives for positive behaviours, which outweigh the financial disincentives for malicious actions.

When the monetary rewards for positive contributions far exceed the possible gains of wrongdoing, why attempt to thwart the system?

Can sovereign states provide and maintain adequate, effective, current legislation, regulation, and enforcement, which synchronises with and benefits the globalised decentralised capital markets community?

In a decentralising global market, they simply cannot.

In proposing this shift in the regulatory approach, it should not be misconstrued as a call for less regulation. On the contrary, it is a push for more regulation. However, the approach is intentionally targeted and prioritises alignment with the interests of the stakeholders that it is designed to protect. Consequently, regulatory goals are fulfilled, and regulated participants do not feel creatively and productively constrained in their positive entrepreneurial endeavours.

21. FROM REACTIVE TO PROACTIVE: REDEFINING THE REGULATORY APPROACH

Reiterating that more regulation, not less, is needed to govern corporate activity, however, that regulation needs to be of a different form and approach in which there is a rebalance between leading and lagging behavioural impacts, that is, a rebalance between cause and effect. The conventional regulatory approach to commercial enterprise inherently focuses on the latter, which limits its effectiveness as it is forever playing catch up to the innovation that it seeks to regulate.

Ingenuity and innovation typically spring from well-intentioned advocates who overlook malicious actors' potential misuse of their creations. Unfortunately, such malevolent entities quickly exploit under-regulated commercial opportunities arriving early at their innovative frontier, corrupting its potential and negatively impacting the fledgling industry. Consequently, based on experience, regulatory bodies and sovereign governments are predisposed to perceive these novel commercial territories with suspicion, which then risks becoming obstructive.

The arduous and costly process of developing reactive regulations, followed by the protracted investigations and prosecutions of those that breach them, will never keep pace with the swift dynamics of commercial activity. While it is necessary to uphold punitive measures, such as fines and imprisonment, corporate regulatory bodies are not equipped to bring justice to all perpetrators of illicit activities. Indeed, regulatory bodies are acutely aware of this, and strategically aim their limited resources to make an example of a select few and hope the threat of potential punishment deters others.

However, this method of instilling fear has repeatedly proven to be a weak deterrent, often leaving malicious entities to weigh the surety of the substantial reward against the probability-weighted risk of punishment. Regulatory bodies might benefit from exploring structures that inherently discourage malicious activities at a commercial level rather than focusing solely on the punitive end of the spectrum. However, the concept of 'regulatory creativity' is itself an oxymoron, since regulations are inherently reactionary and are seldom intelligently devised to prevent behaviour that is yet to materialise.

The question arises:

How can novel commercial activity be regulated effectively from its inception?

A potential solution lies in involving the participants as frontline regulators, thus addressing the imbalance in the numbers of commercial and regulatory participants. Ultimately, the only group that can effectively represent the public interest is the public themselves. 'The public' means 'everyone'. Attempts to elect or appoint subsets of the people to establish, organise and govern regulatory bodies invariably divides these individuals and the broader public interest that they were appointed to serve. Initially formed with a common goal, these regulatory bodies, through natural organisational evolution, often morph into self-serving entities, and the notion of acting in the general public interest becomes opaque in their observed modus operandi. This natural drift towards self-interest is a recurring human pattern where small groups, initially united by a shared passion, unwittingly devolve into self-focused entities.

Therefore, the only group capable of serving as responsible first-line regulators must be the participants, acting in a decentralised manner to pre-empt the emergence of systemic voids that spur the formation of new and potentially unhelpful regulatory regimes. It is in the participant's best interest to operate in a well-governed and trusted environment, as the confidence it fosters attracts more participants. An increase in participants amplifies supply and demand, forming the backbone of efficient markets and optimising their core purpose: which for capital markets is to optimally pair investor funds with entrepreneurial activity for the mutual benefit of each.

Well-formed and understood structures of self-regulation on a global scale are more effectively able to augment behaviour than sovereign-set rules. However, the two approaches can be complementary by each offsetting the inherent limitations of the other. The bureaucratic nature of sovereign government is simply too slow and unaligned to keep in step with the speed of commercial trends and novelty to productively influence behaviours. While the decentralised world, supported by the proper mechanisms, can influence behaviour such that the incentive to do wrong is reduced, it cannot, however explicitly, prosecute malicious actors.

Sovereign nations seeking to coordinate global agreements that will never be able to keep pace in setting an appropriate, comprehensive, timely and enforced legislative framework in the digitalised world. The systemic incentives need to do the heavy lifting with respect to regulating unwanted behaviours. With the speed of commerce and creativity accelerated by the power and array of available technological tools, the utopia of a global legislative framework consensus will slowly recede from societal expectations on the grounds of practicality. However, the outcomes from decentralised processes can be positively augmented by utilising the tools that sovereign governments can wield over individuals.

Another potential approach exists. One that is far cheaper, more efficient, highly practical, and increasingly effective, and it simply requires some novel consideration in its practical application regarding an ordered implementation.

This approach postulates that the online community is the solution. Everyone has a voice, as evidenced by the cacophony of social media, and it may be possible that with the appropriate mechanisms, the commercial world could make better use of this modern phenomenon by building a 'collective conscience' to regulate behaviour.

In commercial transactions, the application of fear and greed often impacts indirect stakeholders, a group that is the largest in number and, given the interconnectedness of global commerce, includes almost everyone and pertinently extends to the natural environment. The directly interested parties in such dealings are relatively few compared to the numerous indirect stakeholders. If given a chance to provide informed feedback, these indirect stakeholders could offer unbiased insights since they bear no direct material consequence from the outcome. However, without any direct exposure, why would they engage in the first place?

Self-regulation is the ideal state for efficiency, integrity, and productivity in any system. The rapidly advancing technical tools for connection, information dissemination, and transactions offer a potential means for enhancing self-regulation. Any system that cannot effectively self-regulate is imperfect and requires improvement for sustainability. 'Self-regulation' suggests an ecosystem that can mitigate the negative collateral impacts stemming from its stakeholders' activities as an inherent function of those same stakeholders' participation. Self-regulation fails when the ecosystem's intended beneficiaries suffer unchecked harm from malicious actors that necessitates external intervention.

Using the human body as an analogy, each part is vested in preserving and optimising the system's health for survival. External medical intervention becomes necessary when the body's natural 'immune system' fails to overcome challenges and restore health. This intervention, while critical, may also cause collateral harm to the system, since it is not a natural part of it. While such interventions may occasionally be required, the body ideally should be capable of avoiding, or otherwise overcoming, its issues independently. The better the body can self-regulate, the healthier, more productive and content it is.

Examining the incumbent systems of capital markets necessitates scrutinising the fear and greed mechanisms and their effectiveness in optimising societal outcomes.

Reputation is an often-underestimated factor which plays a crucial role in these mechanisms, whether it is the reputation of an individual or an organisation at stake. In this context, self-worth, reflected in public opinion, is critical. This doesn't imply that popularity is essential, particularly in the puerile expressions of social media, but rather a comprehensive understanding of the character of the entities one engages with.

A relatable analogy is the selection of one's life partner. Important qualities like kindness, commitment, and honesty, coupled with the genuineness of actions and words, are what most people look for in their partners and the individuals they interact with. A person's character is best understood through their past actions and words.

As Warren Buffet famously said, "It takes 20 years to build a reputation and five minutes to ruin it. If you think about that, you'll do things differently." While it's said that 'reputation is everything,' some individuals care little about others' opinions, pursuing their interests without regard for their indirect stakeholders. For them, the repercussions might include losing friends, job opportunities, or business deals, which may not significantly deter their course of action. Some might operate within a small sphere that meets their needs, often at the expense of the broader community. However, imagine if reputation were more closely tied to the universal price of money for personal and business finance, not only for individuals but also for associated companies or persons. While some might argue that this is already the case, it's clear that current ties are insufficient to suppress the undesirable behaviours prevalent in today's capital markets.

The saying goes, "Money is the root of all evil."

But what if, in capital markets, 'the evil' could be systemically eradicated from money?

What if it were empirically proven that the 'good actors' always achieved financially superior outcomes to the 'bad actors'?

What if global money flows consistently gravitated towards those with the highest-ranking bona fide reputations?

Who would determine reputations—Media outlets? Social media platforms? Government bodies?

If reputational standing held such fundamental importance, developing a nuanced and consistent understanding of what constitutes a 'good reputation' would be crucial as it charters capital markets participation. Public opinion must deliver accurate character assessments. Furthermore, people can change, so any such assessment should be dynamic, reflecting personal growth and transformation. In the age of hyper-information availability, transfer and dispersion, people are inclined to form opinions quickly. Hundreds of good deeds can be swept away by one bad one that is either committed, perceived, or even associated.

Another challenge is that, while each person constantly forgives and 'rerates' themselves for each perceived misdemeanour, people do not like to hold dynamic opinions on others. For most people, on any given peripheral point, the comfort of a galvanised opinion is preferred to a state of constant wonder in perpetually reassessing how they should think about a particular person or idea.

dHowever, they constantly do just that regarding themselves and their 'nearest and dearest'. Because they have a continued relationship with themselves and those they are closest to, they need to figure out how to get along in order to move forward with those they are bound to move forward with. The perceived need for this dynamic approach abates in those opinions that are held for others with whom it is believed that a person will only hold a transitory acquaintance. People are not overly concerned and are well prepared for the anticipated loss of those connections, and thus are under no perceived obligation to constantly reassess an already bestowed opinion.

The move towards the global interconnectivity of everything and, importantly, everyone brings that perception into question. In a globalising society, each participant is part of the wider ecosystem that extends beyond their city, country, culture, language, and worldview. In practice, globalising means interacting and transacting with people across this ecosystem, and to have confidence in doing so, each person needs to have a level of trust in the counterparties with whom they are transacting. In a centralised world, trust is intermediated by brands and structures that become familiar as trust begins with a perceived sense of familiarisation. In a decentralised society, that facilitates more direct interactions, the number of familiar intermediaries will progressively diminish. The requisite trust must be provided by the means of interaction with the counterparties themselves and the knowledge of the counterparties that underpins that sense of trust in the inclination to deal with them.

But who has the time, resources, headspace, and inclination to be constantly assessing what they think, know, and feel about everyone and everything?

In capital markets, as far as listed corporate entities are concerned, this already occurs to an extent. In efficient markets theory, the price of a company's shares at any given time is governed by the universal conclusion of every element that contributes to the company's value, then manifestly applied to that company through the equilibrium point of buying and selling. In other words, every single person can effectively have their say through the buying and selling of shares on the value of that company. Some people will consider the financial fundamentals, others the sector that the company is in, others the individuals involved in the running of the company, as well as a myriad of other factors that are all ultimately distilled to a single number in the form of the share price that represents the value of the company.

Proponents of inefficient markets assert that the market misrepresents the temporal currency of the true value of the company. Consider that this could conceptually arise from having insufficient contributors to the assessment such that each additional contributor gained adds further credibility to the overall average number. Consider if the opinion on a company's value arrived at by one unidentified person should be significantly factored into the opinion of another. Probably not, as the risk that that person is not fully informed is inordinately high, and for ten or even one hundred people, the aggregate competency is still too much of an unknown to conclude that the averaged assessment can be relied on. What about the average assessment of thousands of contributors or tens of thousands or more, each acting independently? The aggregate average starts to become more believable, and the reliance can rise and continue in positive correlation with the number of independent assessments.

In theory, to the extent of price setting, this is equity markets at work with a degree of trust in the floating price set by the forces of supply and demand driven by extensive and broad participation. As demonstrated by the robust, albeit imperfect, nature of capitalism in this regard, for any system to have longevity, it needs to be self-regulating.

Most of the world's population are participants in capital markets from a stakeholder point of view, and very few could legitimately claim not to be. 'The people of the world' are the entrepreneurs, the workers, and the investors, and in this new era, there should be a growing awareness and recognition that they are the regulators as well. If the spirit of self-regulation is to be propagated, the notion of 'regulatory transfer'—that is, that individuals simply seek to shift the accountability of their own missteps to third-party centralised regulators, should be dispensed, as the centralised safety net is becoming patchier and those that choose to rely on it, rather than themselves will at some point find out the hard way that it's simply not there anymore. As it stands and will continue, with increased participation numbers, combined with the speed and adoption of new instruments, the centralised, external regulatory 'safety net' is going to be increasingly more imaginative than real in practice with regard to its ability to limit collateral damage to participants unless it is augmented and assisted by a major lift in the ability of the system to self-regulate.

Accountability is best shared, and the leading edge of market integrity is a matter for the individual participants to help each other to avoid the pitfalls of poor investment propositions, ensuring the world's capital flows to the most deserved opportunities and consequently back to the investors. And, in so doing, produces assets, goods, and services with the most efficient use of global resources to produce the best possible human wealth outcomes in the broadest sense.

The notion of 'Opportunity Equality' resonates strongly with a centuries-old, ever-increasing push towards one of humankind's greatest objectives; 'Civility', which simply means showing kindness to one another. A major prevailing global movement in the pursuit of equality is eradicating discrimination based on birth traits. The equality movement has a long way to go, even to understand the strength and meaning of its own spirit, with most proponents vocally focused on a particular subset of the movement to the potential detriment of other subsets. This is further compounded by the confounding contemporary measure of 'opportunity equality' by 'spectrum uniformity', which unjustly replaces 'historical social discrimination' with 'modern social discrimination' that only serves to leave society with a perpetuating cycle of discrimination.

Will it ever be possible to live without discrimination?

To ensure that true equality of opportunity across all subsets is genuinely aspired to, the varying passions of subset supporters should always maintain a common reference to the greater movement being about completely decorrelating a person's opportunities from their natural circumstances. Just as it seems to be all-permeating in broader society, it is undoubtedly the case in today's capital markets that opportunity inequality is still very real, and worse still, it is structurally maintained.

22. THE QUEST FOR A FULLY INFORMED MARKET: A PURSUIT OF INVESTOR EQUALITY

To recap, an asset listed on a market exchange is exposed to the forces of supply and demand that produce a valuation for that asset determined by the price at which it is transacted. To the extent that the theorem of market efficiency holds, then the resulting market price of an asset reflects the sum of all information, speculation, and other influences meeting at a collective average equilibrium between buyers and sellers at each point in time. This 'market price' is not explicitly tethered to a specific accompanying risk analysis, that analysis, to the extent it exists, is only generally implied in the price action itself. While there are swathes of research and analysis produced by centralised bodies, the landscape of decentralised analysis is scattered, unreliable and difficult to benchmark such that its practical application is limited.

Most active and would-be market participants are not equipped with the skills, knowledge, inclination, and time to undertake detailed, thorough research and analysis for each investment decision. This creates a place for third-party research that users may incorporate into their investment decision-making. However, which third-party research is worth factoring in when, like biased commentators at a sporting match, everyone interested in commenting is likely to have a personal interest that positions them as either inclined to support or berate the strength of the investment case.

Without conflict, however, there is little case for interest. That is not to say that biased research should be dismissed, as without incentive to conduct it, investors would be left with an empty library, rather any research should be consumed by investors in the knowledge of the nature and extent of that bias such that the user can appropriately contextualise the given insights in their thinking.

The market price point produced by the forces of supply and demand will be determined by the perceived risk of future returns and the 'perceived risk' is correlated to 'perceived knowledge'. Consider a person that acts erratically. A stranger that encounters that person may take great surprise at their actions. However, an acquaintance will expect and may even anticipate the actions within their understood nature. If that person had apprised the stranger, then they too would be better prepared, as the observed behaviour, even though unpredictable regarding the individual's actions, is more broadly accommodated in their knowledge of that person, and any engagement, if they chose to have any, would be predicated on that knowledge.

Investment demand is shaped by knowledge, and it is the asymmetries of knowledge that exist within the supply and demand pools in capital markets that, in part, contribute to the creation of profitable buying opportunities for some and loss-making events for others. It must be acknowledged again here that an elementary, though often under-appreciated, fact that there is someone on the other side of every transaction. Whenever someone says that they "had a win" in the market, the consequence is that someone else has experienced a loss through the opportunity cost of not retaining their position.

Some may argue this is simply the way markets function. However, if such an outcome arises due to asymmetry of information access, it violates the spirit of efficient markets. Striving towards fairness and equal opportunity, which fosters confidence and increased participation, benefits all market players. Consequently, the aspiration should be towards a fully informed market. Information asymmetry, wherever identified, must be addressed, as it represents the second-largest structural factor impeding opportunity equality in capital markets. 'Fully informed' does not imply or mandate that each investor is fully-informed. It means that 'the market' collectively is fully-informed. The difference is the availability of information so that each market participant can access it. The extent to which each participant then chooses to consume and factor in that information is a matter for the individual.

'Equity in information access' doesn't exclude the possibility of profiting. Instead, it introduces fairness in the pursuit of profit. Fully informed investors will not all trade identically, given that each person's unique circumstances, life situation, and personal investment strategy will influence their buying and selling decisions. The essential advantage of a fully informed market, which benefits all participants, including investors and entrepreneurs, is the optimal price of capital for human endeavour. Each person's investment strategy will also differ, and within that, the weightings that are applied to the perceived value components of the company will vary.

For example, one investor may rank environmental concerns ahead of short-term financial return, whereas another may not. If a company does not provide sufficient information to allow an investor to properly evaluate the respective value components, then the information gaps are likely to be perceived as higher risk. Information and risk are inversely correlated in investment decisions. Each information gap is an unknown, and unknowns cannot be accurately quantified and thus will default to 'high-risk' classification.

Any inability to undertake a thorough assessment typically results in a lower overall valuation, thus increasing the cost of capital to the company when issuing new financial instruments for funding. While there may be a natural inclination for a company's stakeholders to present the company in the best possible light, any temptation to embellish, to the extent of projecting a misrepresentative profile, is offset by the need for a 'fully informed' market. A 'fully informed' market necessarily includes the full and transparent communication of potentially negative aspects to the valuation components.

Adopting asymmetric communication behaviours should have lasting negative reputational impacts on the individuals concerned that more than offset the allure of potential short-term gains from exploiting asymmetric information trades. This includes both direct and indirect punitive outcomes from the reputational implications. If self-regulating mechanisms within the ecosystem can practically enforce this, the incentive to create information imbalance decreases. Theoretically, it is in a company's best interest to communicate as fully and transparently as possible given its cumulative impact on the average cost of capital.

However, who, even those with the inclination, can absorb information about everything, even if it's available?

Making all information available is a significant step but not the final achievement. The ultimate goal is to use this information relevantly and proportionately in investment and funding decisions. Achieving this requires people power. It necessitates participant collaboration, utilising all available technological tools on a scale capable of meeting the challenge of processing, organising, integrating and delivering all the relevant information on every trading opportunity.

PART VII

A NEW ERA FOR INVESTMENT RATINGS AND THE COST AND AVAILABILITY OF CAPITAL

"We're not gonna sit in silence

We're not gonna live with fear...

Building a Reputation

BB Wolf had recently sophisticated his tastes from pork to property investment. In surveying the green pastures before him, he sought to engage a local builder to assist.

He knew of a few local builders that, through circumstance and now to his convenience, had come to live in the one house. Presenting himself there, he began talking to the first little pig that answered the door. "Little pig", he said, "I am interested in investing in a local builder".

"Well, let me tell you how I go about the process. If you invest in my business, I'll quickly seek to purchase the nearest construction product available in these pastures, which is that straw over there, and I'll have a house built for you in no time.

The second little pig, now calling out from inside, said, "Well, I may take slightly longer and cost a bit more though I can harvest some timber from the adjoining forest and deliver you a sturdier house than my brother here."

The third little pig arrived home from the bank after depositing the rent money from the other two and beckoned BB Wolf to take a step back and look at the house he was visiting. He discussed the various materials and house plans, including the engineering and wind rating specifications of which BB Wolf was impressed.

Later that night, BB Wolf researched the available online information on the builders' past projects. To BB Wolf's amazement, he saw thousands of reviews on the pig's respective historical projects, many at a child's level though others that went into sophisticated detail on each construction, the materials, local planning laws and a host of other pertinent matters. However, he did not possess the background knowledge to discern their significance in his decision-making.

Fortunately, third-party percentage scores for each review allowed BB Wolf, with his limited understanding, to take advantage of the more detailed reviews based on the peer assessments. Further, as the pigs had completed these projects many times over, he could factor in the contemporary views against the historical ones.

BB Wolf concluded that only the third little pig knew what he was doing. Based on reputation, the other two would squander his investment in their flimsy builds that would collapse under the first breath of wind. While the third little pig commanded a high valuation and took longer to deliver, BB Wolf determined he was more likely to realise a return on his investment by having a share of lasting constructions, and to enjoy the steady rental yield given the recent housing shortage in their pastures.

——

23. HARNESSING THE WISDOM OF THE CROWD: A NEW ERA FOR INVESTMENT RATINGS AND THE COST AND AVAILABILITY OF CAPITAL

The price of money is a key driver for global society. The price paid to receive money and the price offered for money is fundamentally linked to the value and prosperity of commercial endeavour, financial wealth, and consequently the potential for the prospect of 'lifestyle freedom'; that blissful sense of owning one's life. Everything slows down when funding costs are high and access is constricted. This type of slowing negatively impacts people's lives through the slower pace of positive advancements in research and innovation, education, consumer choice and prosperity, and thereby living standards. Conversely, when the cost of capital is comparatively low, and access is open, these things move forward rapidly. An economic system prioritising human welfare should seek to bring about the latter.

Consider the entrepreneur who seeks funding, discovering in the marketplace that they must offer their financier a 10% annualised return to secure their desired financing for their venture. To make it worthwhile, the entrepreneur must generate an annual return exceeding 10% on that capital. In turn, the investor aiming to generate a yearly income of $50,000 on their principal of $500,000 must secure an investment yield of at least 10% per annum.

To what extent can the individual investor, and the enterprise receiving funds, influence the price point at which money changes hands?

The determining factor generally lies in the choices available to each party. The fewer alternatives one has, the less likely the resulting pricing will be optimised in the context of the final price point reached through the equilibrium of supply and demand. In conventional capital markets, individual investors typically play a minor role relative to centralised intermediaries in determining the price and availability of business capital. For the most part, individual investors are mere price-takers. The implicit determinant roles of the individual investor and the enterprise in price setting are choked with intermediaries such that neither party comprehends their influence.

Despite significantly more individuals being willing to invest than those working within intermediary organisations within the context of the global population, how can the individual investor be empowered to have a more meaningful say in price setting?

Is a potential framework that could facilitate a standardised crowd-based assessment mechanism for each investment opportunity?

This process begins with examining existing centralised structures and exploring how decentralised networks might fulfil their purpose. Consider commercial bonds, where a bond issuer's credit rating signifies its credit quality in the context of a comparative measure that prospective financiers generally understand. This credit quality translates to a benchmark level of investor confidence that the bond issuer will fulfil their obligations to pay the yield and return the principal.

In contrast, distributed ledger technology invites a community-determined approach, wherever possible, by the overarching decentralised philosophy it enables. It follows that transactions should occur from end to end in a decentralised manner without requiring any centralised parties to intercede. 'Do Your Own Research' is a well-understood and oft-repeated mantra for anyone considering financial exposure to an investment opportunity in the hope of making a profit. However, as noted above, most investors either cannot or do not wish to undertake the necessary research to reach a fully informed decision point, instead relying wholly or partially on the research efforts and opinions of others.

There are only a handful of major global ratings agencies, and their published ratings significantly influence the cost of capital for the financial instruments issued by governments and corporations. However, the resources and interest of these credit rating agencies only extends to a tiny percentage of organisations globally, with generally only the world's largest companies and governments being regularly rated. This leaves most companies excluded from this commercial service, thereby unrated and compelled to counterbalance 'unknown risk' in the market by offering higher returns to attract capital.

The Bond market epitomises the concept of direct 'company to investor' financing within traditional finance. However, due to barriers such as size, regulation, and exchange mechanisms, most of the world's companies and individual investors are excluded from participating directly. Historically, Bond issuance has been the remit of large corporations and investment groups, with most companies left to negotiate with conventional banks or are deemed an unfavourable debt-risk proposition, thus typically directed towards equity-based fundraising.

As confidence in participating in any venture necessitates knowledge, in capital markets, this knowledge pertains to understanding the risk profile of a given opportunity. The few recognised ratings agencies provide this third-party reassurance for investors. Although the rating agencies do not maintain direct relationships with any individual investors, they are familiar and, to a degree, 'trusted'; thus, investors take note of these ratings as a reference point when considering the risk profiles that they are considering gaining an exposure to. For the issuing entity, this results in an observed correlation between the bestowed rating and the market pricing of their bond issues.

Rating agencies are commercial enterprises with the primary goal of generating revenue. While sometimes ratings may be unsolicited, the agencies are generally compensated by the entities that they rate. In engaging with a rating agency, a company must disclose as much information as possible to present a comprehensive view of its business. Like insurance companies, when pricing premiums, rating agencies typically treat information gaps as unmitigated risk areas, as risk calibration can only be ascertained through information analysis. Without all the pertinent information related to a company's value, the rating agency will have gaps in their assessment, which they will associate with a higher risk due to their inability to review and incorporate the information in the overall risk profile.

The paying entity receives value from the rating exercise in the form of an 'independent rating' of its 'credit worthiness', enabling it to go to market with a credible assessment of its probability of fulfilling its debt obligations and thus procure debt at the most competitive price within the market bandwidth for the bestowed rating. The entity may also benefit from the rating process by obtaining a detailed review and benchmarking of its business, which can then be integrated into business improvement strategies aimed at growing and de-risking the business. Success in these endeavours may lead to business improvements for all stakeholders' benefit, helping secure an improved rating and consequently reducing the cost of future finance.

Notwithstanding the conflict of interest inherent in 'who pays whom', the system is conceptually plausible, where the three parties—the enterprise, the rating agency, and the investor—operate with sufficient independence in pursuit of their interests yet find a common benefit, thereby aligning their respective incentives. Rating agencies that are keen to earn their fees are well incentivised to perform their best to secure future assignments. Companies often seek or welcome the opportunity to be rated, as it may aid in obtaining funding at the most competitive price. Investors appreciate seeing their existing and prospective investments rated and will likely weight these ratings in their decision-making. This saves them the time and effort of undertaking or procuring their own research and provides confidence that the investment pricing reflects a benchmarked risk profile.

Much like the imbalance between the number of regulators and capital market participants, there is a glaring disparity between the number of individuals involved in rating companies and the number of companies seeking external finance. This situation perpetuates an exclusivity that, if it were otherwise extended to all companies, could increase the funding and pricing options for finance, and the number and nature of investment opportunities for investors.

How can the beneficial impact of third-party risk benchmarking be applied to a broader array of investment opportunities, stimulating more investment interest via robust market pricing?

The solution lies in widespread participation, for which engagement of the decentralised community is critical. This poses the next series of conceptual questions:

How might one decentralise this synergistic triangular relationship between rating agencies, companies, and investors?

Furthermore, how can every relevant piece of information concerning an investment opportunity be captured, computed, and presented as a quantified and benchmarked risk assessment at any given time?

Encouragingly, some progress has already been made in this direction. However, the existing approaches lack the requisite structure to adequately tackle the above-mentioned challenges. Many online stock forums and social media platforms exist wherein contributors offer their insights and comments with varying analytical depth. Subsequent contributors then evaluate these insights, allowing observers to perceive both the contribution and its peer assessment, thereby gaining a sense of the crowd-driven perspective on any investment case.

The contributor component of the existing online forums for companies is generally peripheral to the purpose of the platform that they appear on. The structure and input of contributions on most platforms are not conducive to condensing all the input down to a single quantitative rating, akin to the rating agency's credit rating, such that investors could be reasonably anticipated to consider and incorporate it in their investment decisions. These forums are generally geared towards listed stocks, though most of the world's companies are unlisted and do not feature in these forums.

Aside from there being no available market to trade unlisted companies another reason that forums overlook them is their lack of information disclosure. Private companies typically prefer to keep their performance data confidential until they require external funding. At this juncture, it becomes advantageous for them to share their story with prospective funders to secure funding on the most favourable terms.

The ability to harness the crowd's wisdom for bona fide investment ratings is integral to the global success of decentralised funding. Transparency and liquidity are the crystallising elements of company value. Transparency means maximum absolute truth at every moment regarding company value. This in turn requires the contribution of the optimal quantity of relevant validated information. Moreover, this information must be presented in a form that is palatable and beneficial to the decision-maker. Liquidity, in its truest sense, denotes the freedom and ability to transact at will, using a value medium acceptable to the transacting parties, which could be cash, but increasingly, in a future where most assets have a digital representation, it may be another form of mutually acknowledged value—such as a Revenue Token.

Is it possible to conceive, implement, and nurture a universal crowd-driven rating system capable of overcoming the barriers to funding and investment, thereby engendering an equitable ecosystem that invites, encourages, and thrives on maximum participation?

24. In Pursuit of Democratic Capitalism: The Universal Crowd Rating

A genuinely democratic, decentralised rating system with sufficiently broad and large-scale participation could identify, consider, prioritise, and amalgamate all factors that society deems relevant to corporate value, thereby directing the cost and availability of global finance and investment. Both individuals and corporations craft brands and social statuses, which can influence how their voiced opinions are received to such an extent that the relationship between 'impact' and 'substance' becomes blurred. Drawing from the wisdom of pre-eminent comedian Jerry Seinfeld, who said that "No one laughs at a reputation," this sentiment should apply to all public contributors. This ensures that each contribution is evaluated objectively, its value incorporated based on its intrinsic merit.

Ambitious strides towards decentralising capital markets, to the degree that substantially supplants traditional centralised intermediaries, necessitate digital technologies and the collaborative endeavour of the global community within a trusted environment. This trust needs to rest in both the contributors and the technology. Unlike centralised bodies, the hard-coded software programming on the blockchain is immutable and is therefore not susceptible to bias or inconsistency over time. Beyond that written into the code, which on-chain is open to be read by all, the code does not have preconceived notions or opinions. It does not fear or benefit from the outcomes it produces. It simply is what it is, which is open, transparent, and verifiable at each point in time.

'The crowd' encompasses everyone—every person in the world is welcome to participate. In an ideal decentralised system, everyone collaborates, united through the public platform operated by its users. The crowd is accountable to itself. Everyone bears responsibility towards one another in maintaining and bolstering the system that underpins global capital markets. Within circumscribed groups, particular interest factions can amplify their advocacies, over-representing their perspectives in the context of the larger crowd. Each individual opinion is valued and should be expressed, recorded, and integrated into the system in alignment with the weightage of those views within that group, with 'the group' being as extensive and diverse as possible.

Ideally, the weightage of each viewpoint should correspond to the number of people resonating with those views, no more, no less. The ability to sway others towards one's opinions should hinge solely on the proponent's transparent, logical, and detailed exposition of their perspective, not their identity, past deeds, or associations. As far as feasible, the proponent should remain anonymous so that each expressed viewpoint is free from preconceived value judgements before being read and evaluated.

Online ratings are already ubiquitous in the consumer domain. Each product and service are susceptible to both biased and unbiased assessments. For instance, a person deciding on a restaurant might verify the venue's online review ratings. Many prospective customers will opt for a rated venue, unwilling to gamble on an unrated experience. If multiple ratings are available, that individual will likely consider and factor the average rating in their decision. Additionally, prospective diners may delve into individual ratings to understand the aspects evaluated by various reviewers. They might consider the number of ratings given and integrate this into their acceptance of the aggregate rating. For establishments or services that evolve, like changes in restaurant management, menu options, and interior design, customers assign more importance to recent ratings than older ones.

If a restaurant only garnered a few reviews, a customer might assign little weight to the average of those ratings. However, if the eatery accumulated 100 reviews, the customer might reasonably deduce that the average presents a reliable guide to what they can expect. The assumption grows stronger with 1,000 reviews and so on. With a larger pool of ratings, customers might skip reading in-depth reviews and instead accept the average rating at face value, assuming the ratings would encompass a mix of thorough and superficial reviews, thus neutralising outliers via the averaging.

Moreover, establishments like restaurants may alter their staff, menus, suppliers, and décor over time, making the experience of a diner from a year ago potentially less pertinent than that of someone who dined there a week ago. This concept of temporal weighting based could extend seemingly static items, such as books or movies, when considering that audience reception may change over time. Many movie releases that fell relatively flat on their initial release have become lauded 'arthouse classics.'

What if the crowd rating system evolved beyond mere aggregation and averaging to incorporate these relevant elements of quality and recency into the ratings?

What if there existed a method to filter and rank the reviews and consequent ratings based on the quality of the review itself and its temporal relevance?

Would such an enhanced average rating be materially useful to consumers?

Consider a simplified dialogue that may have taken place during the inception of Google's Internet search engine:

"How should we structure internet searches?"

"What if we rank them algorithmically?"

Google revolutionised how people access information by deploying an algorithm that organises and ranks information through peer review. It aims to convert the qualitative into the quantitative for the user's benefit.

Similarly, *how should decentralised rating assessments be structured?*

What if they were organised algorithmically?

Systematising an immense number of individual narrative comments, subjective valuation perspectives, and detailed analyses of a given organisation and its performance requires orderly and consistent numerical quantification. This quantification allows for appropriate benchmarking, facilitating reliable comparisons of investment opportunities. The opinion of a single individual on a company might hold little sway within the entire community. However, if 100 people deliver substantiated assessments, the average rating may command some significance, such that its meaningfulness correlates with its participation rate.

To glean comparative insights, an objective grading system must be applied.

But, how can a system claim objectivity when it grapples with subjective matters?

A comprehensive company evaluation involves dealing with both objective facts and intangibles. While historical financial performance and executive remuneration packages can be measured, an executive's motivation level, its influence on their performance, and the impact of their performance on stakeholder-valued metrics are highly material to the performance of the business. Yet they are much more challenging to discern reliably, other than retrospectively, by which time it's too late for the early investor who is already locked in.

Many factors contribute to a company's present value and risk profile. Ultimately, a subjective decision point must be reached. Although this decision point may be informed by careful consideration of facts and insightful analysis, the conclusion remains inherently subjective. Data and information might be objective, but applying knowledge born out of unique experiences leads to individual subjective findings. To approach an 'objective' result with only the 'subjective' at hand requires averaging vast numbers of independent assessments.

Suppose one person assesses an investment opportunity and assigns it a rating of 7 out of 10.

Who can confidently rely on the accuracy of this claim?

How qualified is this individual?

Are they impartial?

How much effort did they put into their research?

It is easier to dismiss the rating by discrediting the evaluator than to genuinely consider the merit of their evaluation. Yet, if ten independent individuals yield an average rating of 6 out of 10, this might carry more weight. The significance grows further if 100 people produce an average rating of 6.25 out of 10. With 1,000 averaged independent assessments, the average rating could play a meaningful role in an individual's decision-making process when considering the investment opportunity.

Nevertheless, the quality of research, information, analysis, and consideration will significantly vary across the rating landscape. With open access, it would be expected that some ratings will lack substantive value while others deliver well-founded, intelligent insights. Ratings from either end of this quality spectrum cannot rationally be given equal weighting in the average. While sheer numbers of ratings may help bell curve the results, it would be a blunt and not particularly useful system that equally recognises and weights the cursory and the considered contributions.

A structured cultivation process is needed to curate the assessments underpinning the ratings, all while maintaining fidelity to the decentralised approach, avoiding reliance on centralised entities. One potential mechanism to achieve this is to apply an averaged peer weighting to each rating. In this way, an informed and insightful rating may receive a peer rating of 8 out of 10, while a superficial rating might score 3 out of 10. The peer review focuses not on the final numerical rating bestowed by the assessor but on the effort, substance, and insights supporting the assessor's rating, as explained in their accompanying narrative. As a result, each contributed rating is individually reviewed by other assessors, and the average rating reflects a substance-based weighting as judged by the crowd.

A third layer of time relevance weighting is then applied to the peer-rated average. When determining the average, the crowd-based rating algorithm should recognise the temporal pertinence of each rating. 'Change is the only constant', and all things being equal, an equivalently substantiated rating from 6 months ago is worth less today than one given yesterday.

The rationale behind creating and administering such an algorithm is that the 'wisdom of the crowd' offers each prospective investor a continually updated risk and return profile of their current or contemplated investment, reflecting the ongoing availability and evaluation of the collective information that the rating community is able to gather. Prospective investors may choose to lightly or heavily incorporate the rating and/or its constituent narratives into their investment theses. At the same time, companies may draw on the evolving analysis and feedback to consider how strategy, operations and communications can be augmented.

Despite having access to information, only a very small number of people have the knowledge, skills, time, and inclination to conduct comprehensive research. This reality is one of the primary reasons centralised intermediaries exist—to inform and advise from a perceived position of credibility. Suppose this postulated triangular relationship—between the company, the rating community, and the investor—takes shape, and the investor can access information in a timely, accurate, and digestible format. It could reduce or eliminate the need for many of the conventional centralised intermediaries in the relationship between the investor and the company by fostering a transaction environment characterised by transparency and trust. While maintaining a symbiotic relationship, the rating providers avoid direct engagement with either the investor or the companies they're rating, thus promoting objectivity and freedom of expression— free from conflict with the subject matter.

25. Calculating and Applying the Universal Crowd Rating

With the concept floated, attention turns to the 'how and why' regarding creating and propagating a here-coined 'Universal Crowd Rating' system. Although the specifics may vary, the Universal Crowd Rating should inherently possess three fundamental components:

1) One or multiple numerically articulated ratings buttressed by a substantiating narrative
2) One or more independent numerical evaluations of 1)
3) A recognition of the temporal relevance of 1)

Components 2 and 3 factor into the averaging of component 1, thereby enhancing the quality as deemed by peer review and the real-time significance of the data. The result of this confluence is a singular Universal Crowd Rating (UCR).

A numerically articulated rating, such as a percentage score out of 100, derives its credibility from an informed and reasoned narrative explaining the rationale behind the bestowed rating. Inherently comparative, the reasoning behind one company receiving a 65% rating and another achieving 72% indicates their relative worthiness as an investment. The criteria determining 'investment-worthiness' is crowd-determined, assessed and ranked. While prospective financial returns may play a part, an assortment of other factors valued by the crowd may also be considered.

The rating system recognises that these factors are subject to change over time and thus the inclusion of the temporal relevance element of the UCR calculation. In addition to the evolving activities and performance of the rated company, many of the factors the crowd deems important will also likely vary over time. The rating community will scrutinise, score, and integrate the sustainability of earnings and operations, environmental impact, community engagement, employee culture, communications, and a broad spectrum of other factors highlighted and presented by the rating community. The average peer assessment of those ratings will determine those factors' inclusion and relative weighting in the overall score. The UCR gains meaning from broad participation and is underscored by the premise of 'wisdom of the crowd'.

Hypothetically, the rating system could apply to any entity, be it a company, product, service, or a range of other items or experiences, where a time-sensitive rating would be meaningful. As a conceptual illustration at a high level, consider the crowd assessment process applied to an investment opportunity. A rating contributor can be anyone that has undergone verification to confirm their unique 'rating contributor code'. They can submit a rating for each investment opportunity at any time and offer multiple distinct ratings at different times.

The rating, expressed as a percentage, gives a quantitative dimension to the assessment, supported by insightful written detail justifying the final percentage rating as the rating contributor deems appropriate. This narrative could range from pages of thorough analytical research inclusive of qualitative insights and rigorous financial evaluation, intending to lend as much substance as possible to their concluding rating, to a shorter piece from an investigative assessor who has unearthed some novel insights that they consider are highly deterministic to the company's standing. This would subsequently be vindicated or otherwise by the peer assessment in the extent to which it is weighted in the UCR.

This second pivotal part of the rating process involves the community 'rating of the rating'. The community in this context comprises individuals who elect to review and score the quality of the rating. Consequently, this generates two ratings: the primary rating and the subsequent peer review, expressed as a percentage score. The 'rating of the rating' method is constructed to promote ratings that possess authentic substance from those determined to have lesser merit. The peer review component recognises that, given the publicly accessible nature of the contributor portal, there will likely be a wide range of quality and insightful depth amongst the various ratings. Therefore, the 'collective wisdom' of the crowd becomes multi-layered, capturing an average quality-weighted rating assigned to each opportunity within the aggregation process.

Reiterating again also that the rating system is dynamic, a necessary quality as the objects being evaluated: companies, products, governments, and other commercial and investment offerings, are also dynamic. Companies perpetually evolve in response to internal decisions and external influences. Consequently, the most recent ratings hold greater weight than the historical ones. The rationale is that the relevance to value and risk of a rating diminishes as time passes.

To encapsulate the above and illustrate the computation of the Universal Crowd Rating for a sample company's investment worthiness, the steps include:

A) A substantiated rating of the company that concludes with a numeric score, which in this example, is out of 100. Notably, this denominator could be 10, 1000, or a percentage to a certain number of decimal places.

B) The average peer-reviewed rating out of 100, as assigned to the assessment in A.

C) The number of days passed since the publication of A, expressed as a percentage of the relative average number of days of other ratings published for that company. A notional expiry date of 100 days is set, beyond which the rating ceases to factor into the UCR calculation due to its diminishing temporal relevance. This notional expiry can be further tuned within the algorithm, if it is deemed excessively long or short.

Although the actual calculation would involve more nuanced intelligence in a real-world scenario, for illustrative purposes, an algorithm for the UCR in its simplest form could be:

UCR = A x B x C

Where:

'A' represents the initial rating.

'B' represents the crowd's average assessment of that rating, divided by the average rating of all ratings for that company.

'C' represents the number of days that have passed since the publication of the rating, divided by the average number of days elapsed since the publication of each rating.

Applying this rudimentary illustrative formula, the table below demonstrates a single average crowd rating (UCR) computation sample.

\multicolumn{8}{	c	}{Example Company UCR}
Credit Assessor	(A) Rating	Avg peer rating	(B) Relative CRA rating weighting	Days since rating posted	Age weighting	(C) Relative Age weighting	Weighted average rating
1	75%	85%	122.74%	1	99.00%	141.13%	1.30
2	72%	95%	137.18%	3	97.00%	138.28%	1.37
3	65%	88%	127.08%	5	95.00%	135.42%	1.12
4	78%	80%	115.52%	7	93.00%	132.57%	1.19
5	56%	65%	93.86%	11	89.00%	126.87%	0.67
6	63%	68%	98.19%	14	86.00%	122.59%	0.76

7	76%	79%	114.08%	17	83.00%	118.32%	1.03
8	77%	84%	121.30%	18	82.00%	116.89%	1.09
9	82%	89%	128.52%	19	81.00%	115.47%	1.22
10	76%	66%	95.31%	21	79.00%	112.62%	0.82
11	65%	45%	64.98%	23	77.00%	109.76%	0.46
12	69%	25%	36.10%	25	75.00%	106.91%	0.27
13	45%	67%	96.75%	29	71.00%	101.21%	0.44
14	65%	64%	92.42%	34	66.00%	94.08%	0.57
15	89%	76%	109.75%	39	61.00%	86.96%	0.85
16	76%	64%	92.42%	43	57.00%	81.25%	0.57
17	54%	38%	54.87%	55	45.00%	64.15%	0.19
18	62%	43%	62.09%	69	31.00%	44.19%	0.17
19	91%	71%	102.53%	73	27.00%	38.49%	0.36
20	84%	93%	134.30%	91	9.00%	12.83%	0.14
AVG	71.00%	69.25%			70.15%		**(UCR)** 72.87%

Reiterating again that the formula used above is merely for simplistic demonstration, and that the application of further statistical tools could augment the outcome. The actual structure of the algorithm, while recognising the circular reasoning challenge inherent to crafting a UCR algorithm from a UCR, should ultimately be a product of a collaborative crowd endeavour to discern and vote on the 'ultimate algorithm' for producing the most efficacious UCR. The UCR should be transparent, its calculation processes open for all to inspect and publicly owned and available. The dilutive and market-confusing presence of multiple UCR algorithms would be counterproductive for the global community of investors and companies who strive to establish a universally recognised benchmark for investment and finance. Any shortcomings or enhancements required in the prevailing UCR should be steered by the crowd, integrating these modifications into the UCR rather than forking into separate rating systems that would dilute the crowd-driven execution and, thus, its participation and relevance.

The UCR integrates quantification and relative benchmarking into crowd ratings. The dual layers of averaging aim to impose order through peer-determined quality verification and temporally relevant filters that instill inherent balance to a decentralised rating system open to contributions from all. The quality check, driven and weighted by peers, is constructed to incentivise intelligent insights over any other contribution which brings lesser value to the primary objective, which is to provide an innovative tool to assist investors and entrepreneurs in decision-making.

The incorporation of time-weighting is critical as it offers currency to the rating, honouring the dynamic characteristics of the full spectrum of value-deterministic elements and the shifting appreciation of the significance and value of those elements over time. For a company, in addition to their internal activities and strategies, it would include the business, social and natural environments in which they operate.

What elevates a rating?

Broadly, it will likely be those ratings that are determined relative to other ratings to have the most insightful, accurate, and substantiated assessment of, for instance, a company's likelihood of fulfilling its obligations to external financiers. Like any prediction of the future, only a retrospective evaluation can determine the accuracy of the rating and the merit of the historical assessment in light of subsequent events. If the system functions optimally, the wisdom of hindsight should help refine future assessments.

It's important to differentiate between the terms 'Rating Provider' (or 'Rating Contributor') and 'Rating Assessor'. The 'Rating Provider' is the individual who initiates the rating, while the 'Rating Assessor' is the one who rates the Rating Provider. A 'person' could be an individual or a team working collectively to submit a rating or an assessment of a rating. Those persons could use whichever tools they wish to deploy, which could, as their sophistication improves, include Artificial Intelligence driven content generator applications. Although publicly anonymous, each Rating Provider and Rating Assessor has a unique identifier for the platform, the importance of which will be discussed in the subsequent chapter.

The system will not explicitly dictate the factors a Rating Assessor may consider. The primary attributes of a company's profile that are given prominence in the rating assessment will be determined by the crowd at every juncture. When rating a company, if the contributing Rating Providers and Rating Assessors collectively decide that net profit is the most vital valuation driver, then that element of company value may take precedence over other factors, such as revenue growth, gross margin, or net asset value. Other elements such as environmental concerns, social justice, or the company's vision and purpose may also be given varying significance levels. Moreover, factors such as employee remuneration structure, executive incentive schemes, the industry's macroeconomic outlook, intellectual property protection, and competition may all vary in rating weight. The crowd will ultimately establish by consensus which key elements are included, and to what degree to rank investment opportunities over time.

In its quest to optimise its goal of bolstering investor confidence and serving as a critical pricing determinant, the Universal Crowd Rating (UCR) algorithm may evolve over repeated application to enhance the governance and integrity concerning the objectivity and insightfulness of its results and fortify it against potential harmful manipulation by ill-intentioned actors. Provided the UCR algorithm is fixed for the temporal relevance period, such as the 100 days asserted in the above example, the algorithm's evolution should not compromise the integrity of the rating system.

Every version of the underlying algorithm aggregating and condensing the ratings into a single rating—UCR—would be open and transparent. This transparency is critical for users to gauge the extent to which they incorporate the UCR into their decision-making. For investors seeking appropriate investment opportunities, this would mean the degree to which the UCR influences their buying and selling decisions. If the UCR plays a significant role in that decision, then, for a given company, the UCR would be a driving determinant of the price at which it can secure funding.

Social media platforms have facilitated billions of people sharing their personal lives by creating an evolving online profile. Similarly, organisations utilise these channels to establish their online presence and interact with various stakeholders—investors, clients, industry peers, employees, the community, and regulators. The concept of the Revenue Token coupled with the Universal Crowd Rating (UCR) system aims to extend this online profiling to facilitate access to and distribution of funds in a decentralised global capital market. The intention is for the organisation's profile, as quantitatively reflected and benchmarked in the UCR, to determine the availability and pricing of external funding.

The UCR is its own concept that could be applied as readily to existing capital market instruments as it is proposed to apply to the conceptual Revenue Tokens. Moreover, the UCR may bridge the flow of investment funds between conventional and emerging capital markets instruments. This implies that the currently elusive and highly subjective concept of 'reputational pricing' becomes direct, transparent, quantifiable, and benchmarked. The Rating Provider requires information to work with, and the more open, current, complete, and refined the information that a company makes available, the more it will be reflected in the accuracy and calibrated output of the rating process in the resulting UCR. The UCR, in turn, materially determines the pricing point set by investor supply and demand, at which the company can access funding. Blockchain verification, which can add value to the perceived trustworthiness of the company's profile components, should also be part of this transparency.

The implications for any organisation defaulting on the terms of their issued Revenue Token, or any other funding instrument that mandates action, derives from the reputational impact that feeds back into the evolving profile of the organisation. This impacts its future UCR, linked to the pricing available for future funding offers. This profile includes the relevant constituent profiles of each promoter, entrepreneur and others associated with the company that the crowd will identify, track, measure and report on through the UCR.

Some people say, "You have to earn my trust", whereas wiser people will say, "You earn my distrust." Companies that do not honour their obligations will 'earn' poor reputations, with the direct consequence being an impact on the future market pricing available for funding. The pricing of a company's future funding requests will factor in the historical record of poor performance in risk and, thus, pricing calculations. This approach should incentivise best practice behaviours as it directly affects the cost of capital for future ventures. Past failure may not mark the end of a career, as corporate redemption is a process. Once the individual, team or company can successfully fulfil their obligations, they may rebuild their 'creditworthiness' over time, thereby reducing their future cost of capital.

Entities that consistently meet their obligations will naturally establish higher ratings and better pricing terms for their new issues, as investors are willing to accept comparatively lower yields for lower perceived risk. As noted earlier, in the market for financial advice, which has been regulated to the point that many people are excluded both from receiving substantive advice as well as access to investment opportunities by the commercial cost/benefit case for advice provision, decoupling the investment thesis from the investor is critical to creating an informed and benchmarked market.

For those investors that have no time and/or no inclination to conduct their own research, they may choose to rest on the UCR alone, knowing that it represents the average of all the people that have chosen to invest their time and talents into the process with their end ratings peer-weighted for both intelligence and temporal currency. Investors, funders or other interested parties that wish to conduct further research can read through the individual analytical assessments underpinning the UCR. Furthermore, they can work through all available information on the given rating subject, and even contribute a rating to the overall aggregation that produces the UCR.

26. Rating Contributor Incentives and Compensation

To cultivate and maintain a critical mass of engagement in the proposed crowd-based rating system, a paramount design consideration is to reinforce the credibility of the UCR mechanism in the manner in which its contributors are compensated through a well-structured, transparent and comprehensive remuneration model.

The credibility of the UCR is either amplified or undermined by the proficiency of the Rating Providers and their consequent vetting. Those whose contributions are deemed most valuable by the crowd should receive higher compensation than those of lesser value. Ensuring that the UCR's overall utility underpins the tangible value of the currency earned by Rating Providers should instill a robust governance incentive for all active participants within the UCR community.

Historically, stock blog sites have amply demonstrated people's willingness to invest their time voluntarily, sharing their insights on specific investment opportunities. Though they might not receive an immediate financial reward, personal interest is a crucial motivator. Some contributors offer an unbiased perspective, aiming to contribute altruistically to the broader investment community. Others may simply be lonely, managing their investment portfolios from their bedrooms, and use these platforms as a social conduit. Some may seek to spotlight the benefits of their investments to convince others to follow suit and thus pushing up the price through increased buying interest. Conversely, specific contributors might underscore perceived flaws in an opportunity with the intent of negatively influencing market prices, hoping to achieve a more appealing entry point.

The reasons for participation may vary, but the impact of individual subjectivity –whether sincere, overenthusiastic, or malevolent—can be mitigated to the point of insignificance by the sheer scale of participation. The magnitude of contributor participation facilitates an averaging process that yields a more objective rating. The UCR aims to achieve this, yet it also necessitates recognition of the efforts of the Rating Assessors through a system of direct remuneration. The combination of direct payment and peer review should further help to strengthen the system's governance.

Rating Providers, given their expertise and interest, are likely to be investors and, consequently, the best-positioned experts to assess a rating. After all, the most competent assessors of ratings are those who provide them, along with the investors who rely on them. Each party has a vested interest in fair rating practices. Investors are indirectly incentivised to uphold best practices as it directly impacts the optimisation of their returns. Any attempts to manipulate the ratings in favour of their current portfolio would be counterproductive, undermining the credibility of the ratings associated with their future portfolio.

The Rating Assessors are incentivized, as it is in their interests to elevate the best ratings such that the associated Rating Providers receive the highest payment, as well as upholding and furthering the integrity of the UCR system.

The impact of Rating Providers that may be either publishing non-value-adding reviews that lack substance, or those perceived as being biased through imbalanced assessments of the available information, should be netted out by the combined effect of the algorithm and the number of ratings.

To maximise the latter, the incentive must adequately encourage the participation of Rating Assessors. Each Rating Provider must receive payment commensurate with the value of their efforts in supporting the system regarding calibrating the risk-return profile for the benefit of investors, as not all ratings are equal. The higher quality ratings, as determined by the Rating Assessors, are more valuable to the accuracy and integrity of the platform. Consequently, payment is algorithmically determined by the average rating assessment of their ratings, with those with a higher average rating paid the most. Consistently higher-rated assessors will receive higher rewards, whereas those that add less value receive less compensation.

To build and sustain the ecosystem, payment should be in the form of a new digital currency that will be here unimaginatively named a 'UCR Token' or 'UCRT'.

Before proceeding further, it is appropriate to pause and reflect on the merit of adding to the rapidly and to date, almost entirely fundamentally unnecessary, expanding universe of crypto assets. Whenever a new digital currency is proposed, its first defence needs to establish why it is necessary in the landscape of existing digital assets. The first defence for the UCRT is the fit for the community.

Why not pay the Rating Providers with an existing medium of exchange, such as a current mainstream digital currency?

The key reason that a dedicated medium of exchange is required is that that dedicated currency is a primary upholder of the integrity of the UCR system. Suppose Rating Providers are paid in a medium that derives its value independent of the UCR community. In that case, the community's actions may influence the amount. However, it does not directly influence the value of the currency that the community receives for their efforts. With a dedicated currency that companies purchase to remunerate the Ratings Providers, the rating community is incentivised to optimally deliver value to those companies and their investors through meaningful ratings.

Rating Assessors who receive, hold, and trade in the dedicated currency – the UCRT—naturally hope that its market value will appreciate over time, particularly given their involvement within the ecosystem. Assuming a fixed supply of UCRTs and continued growth in use due to new and existing organisations availing the UCR system, the market value of the UCRT should theoretically appreciate over time, such that it becomes an asset worth holding for its capital growth potential as well as a medium of exchange.

The UCRT possesses inherent value as it represents the rating fee paid by each company in the market. It serves as both an access fee and an ongoing maintenance fee, paid to secure and retain the services of Rating Providers. This provision of services yields a potential threefold value for the participants:

1. To assist in securing funding

2. To obtain funding at the most favourable pricing, given the global open market's supply and demand dynamics

3. To provide the companies with actionable insights for improvements based on implicit advice and evaluation articulated by the more insightful Ratings Providers.

The UCRT is proposed to be a token traded on the market, which anyone can buy. However, at a functional level, the natural buyer would be organisations looking to attract Rating Providers to establish and maintain a UCR. Like any other currency, the value of the UCRT will be determined by market forces of supply and demand. As discussed earlier, to facilitate its appreciation in value over time in correlation with its growing use, the UCRT would be best served by a fixed issue, meaning that no more UCRT could be created. The only way to acquire it would be to purchase it at the prevailing market price or earn it as a Ratings Provider. While the system grows, a staged release of new UCRTs over several years up to the predetermined limit may be appropriate.

Further automated control, if appropriate, could ensure that the UCRT can be bought on-market but can only be sold once it has been 'earned' by a Ratings Provider. This mechanism would prevent the UCRT from being directly speculatively traded. The buyer must 'spend' the UCRT on ratings, which is its intended use—its utility. If they wish, the Ratings Provider can then sell their UCRTs in exchange for other currencies.

Payment for each Rating Provider that published ratings for a specific company within a defined period will be determined based on the following:

A: Relative Average Rating Assessment for the ratings published by the Rating Provider during the period

B: The number of Rating Providers that published ratings in the period

C: The total amount of UCRT available for that company for that period

D: The Aggregate Average Rating Assessment for that company for that period.

The basic formula to calculate the payment due to each Rating Provider is as follows:

UCRT payment = ((C/D) x (1+(A-D)) / D))

To illustrate this with a simple example, consider a company for which 20 Rating Providers published ratings within a defined period. The company had accumulated ten UCRTs available for distribution in the period.

RECAPITALISM

Rating Provider Remuneration		
Ratings Provider	Avg Ratings Assessment (A)	UCRT Paid
1	78%	0.60
2	84%	0.64
3	65%	0.50
4	59%	0.45
5	76%	0.58
6	96%	0.74
7	44%	0.34
8	51%	0.39
9	53%	0.41
10	46%	0.35
11	23%	0.18
12	65%	0.50
13	93%	0.71
14	98%	0.75
15	87%	0.67
16	67%	0.51
17	45%	0.35
18	26%	0.20
19	61%	0.47

20 **(B)**	86%	0.66
Aggregate Average Ratings Assessment	65.15% **(D)**	
UCRT Balance **(C)**	10.00	

Applying the formula to the given data to calculate the due payment for Rating Provider 1 gives:

UCRT = ((C/D) x (1+(A-D)) / D))

= ((10/20) x (1+(0.78 − 0.6515) / 0.6515))

= 0.6 UCRT

While the above illustration serves as a starting point, variations will likely be observed to enhance the integrity of the results and deter manipulative attempts. Such adjustments could include the following:

- Only incorporating Rating Providers who achieve an average Rating Assessment above a certain threshold, thereby discouraging frivolous contributions.

- Altering the UCRT period, potentially lengthening by two or threefold for new Revenue Token issues, in line with the percentage order of magnitude applied to the Revenue Token issue event.

To bolster the system's integrity, the identity of the Rating Provider authoring the rating should remain undisclosed. Rating Providers are not meant to be 'Influencers' beyond the fundamental peer-assessed value of each rating they produce. This measure ensures it is the rating that is peer-reviewed, not the Rating Provider.

Granted, this aspect of author identity connected to successive ratings might be easily circumvented through similar writing styles and other implicit identifiers within the ratings. However, suppose a Rating Provider purposefully indicates their identity. In that case, they might risk being marked down by their peers, who recognise this intentional violation of one of the system's integrity components.

As noted in the last chapter, the need for verifying each unique Rating Provider on the platform is essential for two reasons:

1) To acknowledge them as the official authors for payments.
2) To prevent them from rating their own ratings.

While AI-driven tools will no doubt be utilised by Rating Providers, for the reasons above, it's important that the resulting rating and its supporting analysis are tied to a person (or an organisation) that has created or deployed these tools, albeit that this book is being written at a point in time such that this conceptual prerequisite may become redundant in future.

The decentralised crowd rating system—IUCR system— has potential universal application and is not limited to companies with an active or pending Revenue Token offering in the market. Any organisation can participate if it offers adequate UCRT to maintain the interest and efforts of the rating community. Both corporations and governments currently invest significant resources in investor relations in various forms to attract and retain investor interest. Furthermore, organisations generally value research reports as they provide an external and perceptively unbiased analysis and summary of the investment case. Through these efforts, organisations aim to optimise their valuation and consequently favourably influence their cost of capital.

However, company research in the conventional capital markets system is rarely wholly unbiased. Commonly in capital markets, research is either directly commissioned and paid for by the company or procured by an associated party, like an invested brokerage research department or an engaged investor relations group. The UCR system provides for a more systematic, accessible, comprehensive, benchmarked, and truly objective approach.

For investors, undefined risk is one of the main deterrents to investment opportunities. With a properly functioning decentralised UCR system at critical mass, risk can become more definable, measurable, and benchmarked globally, thus broadening everyone's investment and funding horizons.

PART VIII

THE RISE OF DECENTRALISED CAPITAL MARKETS: COEXISTENCE, EVOLUTION AND LATERAL DISRUPTION

"This time, we know we all can stand together

With the power to be powerful...

Pulling the Sprout to Make it Grow (Chinese Proverb)

Once upon a time, a farmer had recently planted a new crop in his field. He surveyed the young sprouts with great satisfaction as they emerged from the soil. Each day, he would carefully measure the sprouts after having watered and fertilised them and removed the weeds that grew so they didn't rob any nutrients. Day after day, he tended and cared for his crop, and although he could see that the sprouts seemed healthy, he became frustrated at their growth, as it was too slow for his liking. He had prepared the field and given them everything they needed to grow big and strong, though they just weren't growing as fast as he thought they could.

Frustrated, the farmer pulled at one of the sprouts and saw it emerge a little more from the ground. Delighted, he began tugging on each sprout ever so gently, just enough to yield a little further. After he had worked across his field, he surveyed it with great pride, seeing that, finally, each sprout was standing noticeably prouder. The farmer returned to his cottage very satisfied with himself, and intent on returning daily to be the instrument of their augmented growth.

That night at the dinner table, the farmer proudly told his family about the progress of his field and what he had done to the sprouts to encourage them. Distressed, his

ADAM GALLAGHER

son excused himself from the dinner table and ran out to the field with a light to examine the sprouts. To his dismay, he saw that most of the sprouts lay wilted and withering, and, alas, the first crop in the new field was ruined.

——

27. Three Pillars of Novel Financial Instruments: Issuers, Investors and Marketplace

Making a compelling case for a global recalibration of corporate ownership and shifting price-setting power to a decentralised community necessitates an equally robust plan of action to support such a potential revolution. Any novel financial instrument requires three foundational elements to launch:

1. Issuers
2. Investors
3. A marketplace

To sustain growth after its initial launch, the following supplementary factors must also be present:

- Defined operational parameters
- Marketing
- Distribution

For long-term, sustainable growth, the instrument should also demonstrate the following:

- Capability for product evolution
- Potential for new market expansion
- A distinct competitive advantage

These additional elements will evolve naturally once the instrument has been successfully launched. However, for Revenue Tokens to exist, they must hold sufficient appeal for issuers, such as companies, governments and other organisations, and investors. This appeal should manifest in the form of benefits that exceed that which participants might otherwise achieve through alternative financial instruments that are currently available.

While open to all, in practice, the initial issuers of Revenue Tokens are most likely to be companies rather than governments or other organisations due to their number, need and willingness to explore new financial instruments. Small businesses searching for external funding, particularly those in the early stages of their journey, often have few options other than issuing new equity and diluting their existing ownership base. Those that ultimately succeed in reaching their ambitious business goals may retrospectively consider their initial equity issues during their developmental stage as a staggering cost of capital, given their subsequent value appreciation.

Consider a small company raising $200,000 at a $1m valuation, which subsequently achieves a $100m valuation in future years. The effective cost of that initial $200k funding round at that future valuation is $20m. Granted, this example is overly simplistic. It can easily be argued that the high-risk accepted by early investors when injecting the $200,000 are justly rewarded for their "all-or-nothing" investment in a high-risk early-stage venture, where it may have otherwise resulted in a total loss of their principal. However, early-stage companies often find themselves caught in a restricted supply and demand environment for capital, resulting in a skewed pricing mechanism. These companies must accept the investment terms dictated by a limited number of willing parties, given that they are not listed on a public market and do have the means to effectively promote their story to a broader audience of investors.

If there were a larger pool of funding suppliers, then the company would have more choices and potentially be able to secure monies on better terms. Furthermore, suppose they had a funding instrument available that could be more finely tuned to meet their anticipated requirements regarding the provision of adequate funding, and presenting the prospect of a sufficiently attractive return for investors. This would likely put these companies in a more commanding position to optimise their funding arrangements.

The ability to 'tune' the one instrument in the Revenue Token for the company's specific needs at any given time makes for a dynamic instrument that can conform to the pricing calibrations which may be made possible in a well-populated supply and demand pool. For example, an early-stage company for a given purchase price may issue a Revenue Token that allocates 5% of its cash inflows from revenues, and if it occurs, the proceeds from the sale of the company for five years post the issue of the Revenue Token. After five years, the token expires and the company has no further obligation to the investor, and the associated cash inflows return to the company. Why might an investor opt for this? Like any investment opportunity, it would hinge on pricing and expected return.

If each token were valued at $1 and projected inflows over the five-year term were $5, this might represent a fair investment, subject to the risk profile. The risk profile would be gauged from the effective functioning of the rating community, conferring a single, dynamic, and comparable UCR on each investment opportunity. Once issued, the Revenue Tokens trade on decentralised exchanges at the current market price, which would fluctuate according to the market's perceived consensus view of the future performance of the issuing company. Investors could thus buy and sell based on their valuation perception at the market price, receiving the applicable yield in accordance with the issue terms while holding the RT.

As the expiry date draws near, the value of the RTs would likely fall to match or trade at a discount to the remaining anticipated yield to be received until expiry. At this point—or indeed at any point—the issuing company may reach a 'buy-back price position', whereby the market price discount on future yield is less than the value of those foregone revenues to the company. Consequently, the company may attempt an early on-market buy-back of the tokens.

The dynamic nature of Revenue Tokens invites utilisation of the instrument by any organisation, including larger companies and governments, in the same manner that other participants utilise them. The difference will be in the pricing. The pricing encompasses all aspects of the structure of the Revenue Token that are broadly categorised into the yield and the term. Each of these two characteristics is initially calibrated to optimise the funding requirements for the issuer and the return requirements for the investor that is ultimately expressed as the price point reached in the marketplace through the progressive offering of the Revenue Token by the issuer up to the price-point that demand for the token issue is exhausted. Following the initial issue, the subsequent pricing is determined by the secondary marketplace of buyers and sellers.

For investors, once the Revenue Token instrument is adopted by a broad spectrum of businesses across risk profiles, geography and industry, the instrument should appeal to the most risk-averse through to the most risk-aggressive investors. Within that, there will be a wide range of issuing organisations, from the lowest perceived risk opportunities that, as a consequence of their perceived safety, offer lower yields to investors relative to their purchase price, right through to the more 'bluesky' prospects of receiving yield that may ultimately prove to be in multiples of the initial purchase price. Within this market, investors can select a risk/reward position to suit their investment objectives. As more issuers enter the market, investors should be able to overlay their preferred risk/return expressed as percentage yield and UCR range and be presented with a list of Revenue Token opportunities that match their investment profile.

Contrasting this hypothetical scenario, contemplate the complexity and inefficiency individual investors have historically faced in attempting to replicate this process. The conventional centralised approach is comparatively time-consuming and cumbersome, as advisors must take their clients through a web of compliance-driven processes to manufacture specious circular risk profiles that align them with the narrow field of centrally approved investment opportunities.

Currently, individuals opting to invest directly cannot easily access a global array of direct investment opportunities and far less establish a reliable risk profile that supports their assessment of the pricing and its appropriateness for their situation. This necessitates the involvement of intermediaries, introducing further layers of trust, cost, and complexity and diluting the financial benefits for the two key capital market players: investors and companies. These challenges similarly confront companies seeking external finance, leading to fewer ventures, thereby perpetuating the participant deficit and thus diminishing the outcomes in the interactive forces of supply and demand.

Envisage a future where Revenue Tokens have achieved widespread adoption, enabling investors to finely tune their risk/return appetite in increments of percentage fractions from a global catalogue of opportunities, each benchmarked by their respective UCR. With its unique risk profile, each issuer would offer a return determined by market forces, presenting a universe of accessible investment choices. For illustrative purposes, consider a range of opportunities displaying calibrated returns for arbitrary examples of 3.4%, 6.8%, 10.2%, 17.8%, 32.1%, 58.6%, and so forth, extending from triple-digit ultra-high relative risk-return multiples to near-zero risk propositions such as stable government bonds that only promise principal preservation or still less in real terms. Consistent with the core tenets of investing, all opportunities would be underpinned by a market-assessed risk/return proposition influenced by the forces of supply and demand.

For these transactions to occur, willing issuers and investors require a platform. Revenue Tokens must be readily exchangeable, as liquidity is a prerequisite for investors and aids in setting a consensus price driven by supply and demand. As a digital asset, and consistent with the mantra of decentralising capital markets to the maximum extent, the existing and future decentralised exchanges are the natural preferred transaction points for the Revenue Token market. Exchanges should not be centralised at any level, including the legislative or geographic. Doing so limits their effectiveness, which is defined by fairly optimising the valuations of the investment opportunities listed on the platform. Every other element of an exchange, including listing rules, governance, trading processes, information flows, and promotion, feeds into this simple principle. Exchanges should be distributed, objectively programmed, and crowd-governed.

A 'regulation by incentive and programming' thesis should be consistently adopted to underpin compliance with systemic 'good behaviour' inherently incentivised, and 'bad behaviour' disincentivised. Malicious undermining of the system should be prohibitive at a risk/reward level through commercial mechanisms that govern the price of money through the effective functioning of the UCR. Market access is available to all at a price that reflects the issuer's probability-weighted return. There is sufficient funding in the world to fund every worthy business venture at the expense of every unworthy one. It just needs a platform that invites it.

28. THE UCR: BRIDGING PROFIT AND REVENUE-CENTRIC PARADIGMS

Four fundamental factors must be acknowledged and upheld to complete the blueprint for this innovative launchpad. The following essential elements are required for this hypothetical transformation, assisting issuers and investors in transitioning towards a decentralised approach to investment and finance:

1. Dissemination of knowledge,
2. Definition and automation of processes,
3. Implementation of borderless regulation, and
4. Transaction of value.

This approach isn't about directly challenging the established norms. Instead, it signifies a lateral disruption to the traditional, centralised institutions by presenting an alternative pathway. The novel approach will likely gain traction if it can demonstrate its ability to generate and access capital with lower overall risk, a more extensive choice, superior returns, and equality of opportunity for all participants.

Pragmatism consistently offers the most effective path for the longevity of any competing philosophical movement. Therefore, it's advantageous for any emerging paradigm to evolve alongside the incumbent one. This coexistence provides an opportunity to display its comparative merit, which, in this case, arises when investors and companies determine the financial instruments that best fulfil their needs. Technology has bestowed an invaluable gift on global commerce that surpasses even the phenomenal information access and convenience made possible by the internet. This gift, as discussed in earlier chapters, is 'Trust'—a brand of trust unlike ever before. It's trust that doesn't necessitate a bridge of belief for its subscribers. It's trust manifested in the form of verifiable and immutable programmed records enabled by blockchain technology.

Applied judiciously, blockchain technology can bridge the trust chasms that have historically existed between transacting participants. In the past, these gaps were filled by an expanding network of intermediaries, including regulators, professional service providers, brokerage firms, and centralised exchanges. Each of these entities, with their unique suite of fees and processes, traditionally stood between the investor and the enterprise, inevitably diluting the purity and potential of what can now be instated.

In this context, 'purity' refers to the efficiency of time, cost, and effort, along with eliminating barriers to entry. The proposed approach encourages the full spectrum of ready supply and demand participants for each opportunity. The historical absence of systemic trust in marketplaces, combined with the efforts to attain it, led to layers of checks and balances. Unfortunately, these layers affected the market's access, participation, and efficiency of outcomes. Systemic trust, however, enables the realisation of a utopian state of sustainable marketplace purity.

Furnished with information, convenience, and now trust, the only missing ingredient to start taking great leaps forward in enterprise financing and truly democratising investment is quantified knowledge. To underpin pricing and investment decisions, the UCR system seeks to provide this. The Revenue Token concept is proposed as a new complementary financial instrument that seeks to facilitate the exchange of value between investors and enterprise with collateral benefits to the holistic wealth of individuals, wherever and in whichever capacity they choose to connect with global capital markets.

With the tools in hand, the paradigm shift from centralisation to decentralisation can start in earnest, passing through the great mountains of cultural inertia and the waves of 'incumbency revolt' that any new paradigm must navigate to displace the old one. Centralised bodies, and particularly the most developed sovereign states, will likely erupt against the decentralisation of capital markets. Empires, in their many different forms, all have an instinctive allergic reaction to decentralisation as the notion appears to threaten the erosion of the power that sustains their existence. Notwithstanding the systemic relief that decentralising provides centralised bodies from the growing challenges of their remit. However, as this paradigm contemplates the cost and availability of money, once the process starts, it will only gather pace as people will never willingly seek less trust, productivity, convenience, less choice, and less prosperity.

Beyond incumbency and cultural inertia, the price of money can drive growth in the new era for capital market participants. If a company seeking to raise $1 is faced with a choice between it costing 1c or 5c, all things being equal, the company will take the 1c option. If all things are not equal and the 1c option is also faster, more reliable and increases perceived future value, then the decision becomes even easier.

In recent years, the telling indignancy of dismissive arrogance expressed by the bewildered stakeholders in incumbent centralised bodies that "people have lost faith in institutions" is symptomatic of the early phases of the great change afoot. A void is being created by the turning shoulder of the collective conscious as it rejects the notion of faith-based belief in capital markets institutions, both public and private, in favour of basing decisions on knowledge derived from objective, transparent and verified information. The void exists as commerce, particularly investment, is still largely controlled by the centralised bodies of government, central banks, stock exchanges and institutional funders. None of these groups are inherently bad, however, they are not inherently good either, and they should face perpetual merit-based assessment just like everyone else. No entity deserves the sustained presumption of competence without continued demonstrated merit.

Presented with choices, the global community should not be or feel coerced into allocating their discretionary investment spend through intermediating entities if they do not want to, any more than they are compelled to utilise decentralised alternatives. Each investment opportunity should simply stand on its own comparative merit. Centralised entities can certainly participate in the new world, and, with the depth of their financial and talent resources, they should do that very well. However, they will no longer be able to set the cultural rules of engagement, they will have to play by the rules set by the global community of participants.

A decentralised system that's equitable, accountable, and dynamically developed by the global community minimises by design the excessive influence of minority interest groups. In this system, the popular majority determines the lay of the land. Minority groups will continue to be heard, possibly louder than before. Still, their ability to sway outcomes will be proportionate to the global community's average assessment of their views. No longer can a small elite infiltrate centralised governing institutions, regulatory bodies, and funding sources and wield power over mainstream outcomes disproportionate to their supporter base. Like everyone else, they must garner a support base with the rational weight of their arguments.

The move to tokenise gross cashflows, rather than net cashflows, is a fundamental shift, as it opens the door to balanced ethical decision-making in capital markets, which could be one of the greatest systemic elevations of humanity. The soft start to the transition is in sharing knowledge via the implementation of the UCR platform, which can be established and operate independently of the Revenue Token platform. Aside from the direct vested interests of the few participating centralised agencies, the UCR platform seeks to disrupt, decentralise and vastly improve the effectiveness—and thus the usefulness—of one of the less considered, though highly material, pillars of the current capital markets systems.

In the face of machine-automation, while incorporating the best of technological tools, the UCR may be an area of sustained human professional longevity. Sorting through the numbers is the easy part of the analysis. Artificial Intelligence can pull the available information, examine the numbers and trends, benchmark against other companies and indicators, and provide predictions based on that analysis. However, when it comes to forming views on the likely performance of individuals and strategies, the back history of data is often less relevant, and the conclusions formed stray more into subjective reasoning, which, while it may be AI supported, is likely to remain a human-directed domain for some time yet.

In isolation, Artificial Intelligence algorithms risk applying unfair metrics to otherwise robust organisations based on aggregated demographic or geographic statistics if the UCR process were to become fully automated. The UCR system aims to be as objective and fair as possible, presenting each assessed opportunity purely on crowd-determined merit. Since organisations are essentially groups of individuals, a fully automated assessment will never capture all aspects. An array of individuals, aided by digital tools in their work and the coordination of that work, stand a better chance. In this vein, major technology companies have demonstrated a degree of caution when developing AI-driven financial profiling for individuals. The reasons behind this hesitation are equally applicable to the potential profiling of organisations.

The UCR system does not dictate the content of the ratings. This determination rests with the Rating Providers and the Rating Assessors. The algorithm driving the UCR merely strives to organise the diverse opinions of the participating individuals.

The most formidable task lies in supplanting an incumbent, albeit imperfect, structure with a new one. An alternative approach involves constructing and presenting the latest design in parallel, contrasting it with the old, aiming to coexist rather than overtly disrupt and displace. The UCR, as a universal rating system, can help facilitate this transition between paradigms, providing a bridge for entrepreneurs and investors to navigate between profit and revenue-centric paradigms, as it is aptly applied to each.

For larger organisations, obtaining a conventional credit rating from a recognised rating agency is standard practice, and the bestowed rating significantly influences the price at which the organisation can raise funds. Likewise, suppose a UCR has the same impact. In that case, any organisation looking to raise external funding, irrespective of the funding instrument, will likely see the benefit in maintaining a current UCR, as the cost/benefit case is clearly linked to the price of capital. As the market acknowledgement of decentralised ratings increases, funders may begin to require organisations to maintain a UCR, and this approach starts to become a common feature in the dynamic profile of each market participant.

29. ACCOUNTABILITY IN THE DECENTRALISED REALM: MASTERING DESTINY

Approaching the decentralised era with a centralised mindset poses the greatest risk of squandering the opportunity. After millennia of trending towards it, the 21st century is starting to see the tide receding on the prevailing paradigms of centralisation in commercial and social interaction. Sovereign governments, and the centralised institutions under their jurisdiction, cannot be expected to lead, comprehend, and less so, welcome the decentralised movement. The pillars of the centralised era may either take a resistant position and wield their perceived strengths to limit it, or, by contrast, the forward-thinking ones will apply their actual strengths to seek to positively shape it.

Governments are not directly responsible for what happens to participants in the decentralised community. Provided it is not caused by these bodies running interference, the old-world institutions cannot be held accountable when things go wrong. In moving forward, the greatest opportunity and the greatest fear is that the swelling undercurrent of decentralised participants will each have to acknowledge that they are the masters of their own destinies. The recourse for self-sabotage is not as secure as it is, or otherwise perceived to be, under the comforting yet suffocating blankets of centralised control.

This burden of accountability for one's actions and words accompanies freedom and choice. One of the great 'reasons for being' for centralisation is recourse: the ability to blame someone else and seek compensation when things go wrong. Recourse is necessary when breaches of trust occur, and centralised models are littered with that.

However, when trust is absolute, the channels for recourse diminish, and participants are increasingly left with exclusive ownership of the outcomes of their decisions. Success in business and investment always has been down to the individual. The tides of institutional fear and greed have built and washed away many companies with valuations built predominantly on misplaced market confidence. Clearing the webs of intermediaries from the system by bringing crowd-driven clarity may reduce the amplified nature of trends that swing independently of fundamental value. However, the individual must make their own, albeit with the UCR better informed, risk/return-based decisions.

This is the sting in the tail of the decentralised approach, in which each party is accountable for their own decision-making. Participants must also acknowledge their accountability to take willing steps into a system that provides absolute trust in the process. In the conventional system stacked with centralised intermediaries, participants are wedded to the concept of recourse. Information is opaque, and the landscape is strewn with structural conflicts of interest through the misalignment of incentives and regulatory parameters that seek to straighten the structurally twisted.

In a decentralised system, where the structure is programmed and every effort is made to align incentives to desired outcomes at every level, the available information is as complete, pure, and digestible as possible. The mirror is then held up to the decision-maker, and the scope for legitimate recourse when things go wrong is diminished. However, any societal system would be imperfect if it were to leave it at that. Thus, the Rating Assessors' crucially enabling role is to take all available information, analyse it, and condense it down to a rating that facilitates calibrated decision-making. The decentralised approach can deliver a system that presents an ocean of new investment and funding opportunities.

The UCR system is designed as a tool of convenience for investors. Ultimately, it will always remain 'Buyer beware', and that buyer will neither know the UCR participants nor have legitimate recourse or entitlement to reparation as the UCR operates independently of individual investor transactions. The integrity of the UCR system is maintained by a self-governing ecosystem, such that its existence and growth depend on the aggregate value it provides investors.

Even at maximum take-up, with all the available information on each investment opportunity accessible to every investor and in a manner that can be reduced to a simple numerical rating, the investor must still ultimately make their own decisions. Similarly, the finance-seeking company must decide which money to take, at what price and when. The company must exercise skill and diligence in developing and launching its investment offering otherwise, it may experience suboptimal financing outcomes.

While this track may create a perceived re-opening for advisory groups in the new era that could provide legitimacy for centralisation in the decentralised world, it does not. Advisory services can also be decentralised. Similar to each company offering full disclosure for the purpose of assessment to determine the pricing of money, each individual can do the same if they wish. If they do not want to spend time reviewing investment opportunities and building out their individual portfolios, then the crowd can propose it for them. For example, individuals could anonymously open their financial profile and investment inclination for public assessment and receive a peer-reviewed diagnosis of potentially suitable investment portfolios. Similarly, companies could receive continuous and 'free' corporate advice by drilling down on the narrative rating assessments that ultimately determine their bestowed UCRs over time.

While the UCR system potentially opens a new era for information, guidance and implicit advice, it does not necessarily need to enter the market as a combatant to third-party advisors. While historically, the intermediating agent is required as the individual does not have direct access to the information and the opportunities. In the decentralised era, the individual has the information and the opportunities at their disposal. However, they may choose to involve an agent. The notion of choice is key in an equitable and fair system with equal access to all information and opportunities. Those same third-party advisors can assimilate with the rating community to continue to apply their knowledge and experience in return for a commercial reward however, the rating community levels the field, and the advisor will not be elevated beyond the merit of their contribution. Only those advisors who excel at what they do will be justly recognised and rewarded for the value that they provide.

30. REDEFINING CAPITALISM: A 'HUMAN-CENTRIC' APPROACH

Addressing, or perhaps more accurately, 'redressing' the unintended diminishment of human welfare resulting from the existing application of capitalism—Icentred around the ownership of net distributed cash flow—requires a shift from idle speculation to tangible action. However, established incumbents, behaving like the biological immune system, efficiently expel foreign concepts threatening the profoundly entrenched and invested status quo. The subtle and parallel introduction of new ideas to the receptive market fringes is often the best entry before more boldly attracting and consolidating existing participants.

Strategic, sequential small steps within a broader changing philosophy that progressively unveils in synchrony with incremental practical adoption will always surpass strident, ideologically charged onslaughts in their net success. No one appreciates having their firmly held beliefs dissected. However, if presented with attractive alternatives as choices, the perceptual defensive barriers are lowered. This, in turn, permits the incumbent and the novel strategies to be more evenly subjected to objective, merit-based participant comparisons.

'Recapitalism' is a social movement with an economic foundation, striving not to supplant but to enhance the holistic concept of human wealth. This idea of wealth extends beyond the purely financial and looks to the greatest societal aspiration of civility, articulated through the aspiration for the equality of access and opportunity for fostering positive human endeavour. The ten steps along the Recapitalist journey that transition from introspection to action can be succinctly proposed as follows:

1. Recognise
Acknowledge the formidable strengths of capitalism in leveraging the primary motivators of human behaviour via financial incentives to innovate while concurrently recognising the collateral societal damage stemming from the prevailing 'for-profit' focus of currently applied capitalism.

2. Rethink
Contemplate alternate approaches that conserve and expand the positive attributes of the capitalist system in promoting human endeavour, yet strive to mitigate the potential for resultant collateral societal harm.

3. Reinvent
Innovate by utilising available technologies to augment capitalism.

4. Redefine
Reformulate capitalism via a new, lasting human-centric approach where a comprehensive rating system supplants the singular 'for-profit' metric. The UCR system should strive to assess, integrate, and reflect the full societal impact of any given enterprise in its resultant UCR.

5. Redistribute
Diversify the flow of value by establishing a level playing field for all participants through disintermediation and unrestricted access. This access should be borderless, dynamic, and direct, thereby ensuring equality of opportunity for both initiators and supporters of enterprises.

6. Reinvigorate
Reenergise capitalism by freeing finance from all aspects of exclusivity—geographic, scale, education, networks—and bring opportunities to everyone. This enables and empowers a new and sustained wave of global and positive 'hyper-innovation' by providing the necessary means and incentives.

7. Recapitalise
Recapitalise at the revenue level and synchronise investment interests with the interests of all stakeholders, offering them the potential for the most comprehensive concept of wealth—the profound fulfilment of individual potential.

8. Rebuild
Rebuild society through the aligned positioning of institutions, wealth, innovation, livelihoods, and lifestyles.

9. Redress
Rectify the harmful collateral damage of the historical approach on the 'wealth' of individuals, society, and the environment. This can be achieved by applying a more comprehensive, sophisticated, calibrated, and

collectively determined financial value to enterprises that best reflects their potential to serve both the individual and the common good.

10. **Recapitalism**
Recapitalism materialises through efforts to create and cultivate compelling monetary incentive mechanisms, which deliver enhanced social outcomes for all stakeholders and society at large through their operation.

To further distil the essential tenets of the Recapitalism thesis, a metaphoric acronym of a D.I.E.T. might be drawn on, where each element provides a crucial nutrient poised to reshape and re-energise the health of capital markets:

Democracy, in this context, is not akin to the kind frequently manipulated in Western politics. Instead, it represents a genuine definition and application in capital markets. Here, individuals don't merely have the right to voice their opinions—they have a merit-weighted say, as evaluated by their peers.

Inclusivity, where the maximisation of participants with a systemically equalised opportunity, is prized in every sphere of enterprise and investment.

Efficiency is realised through adopting and cultivating technologies and business cultures that eliminate all unnecessary intermediaries. This approach ensures a more direct connection between the actual value endpoints: the enterprise that creates something of value and the individual investors who seek exposure to it.

Transparency is secured by maximising the accessibility of knowledge, coupled with the transparent curation and summarisation of information throughout the decision-making process. Making relevant data available enables informed decisions based on clear, unobscured insights that improve outcomes for investors and investees.

Embedding the D.I.E.T. approach to reforming capitalism would help to right-size capital markets by removing excess exclusivities that currently restrict the freedom of innovation, finance and investing.

Recapitalism: The Manifestation of a New Capitalist Paradigm

Recapitalism champions the cause of maximising democratic participation in both entrepreneurship and investment. It promotes this principle by fostering equal opportunity facilitated by a system governed by incentive-led decentralisation. In this proposed shift, decentralisation is not merely a concept but an intrinsic system characteristic. It postulates a future where only three fundamental roles exist across the entire spectrum of enterprise and investment: Entrepreneurs, the Rating Community, and Investors.

The role of the Entrepreneur is not confined to those who launch companies. It includes all working within these companies, recognising their contribution to the entrepreneurial endeavour. These individuals form the backbone of value creation, bringing new ideas, products, and services to life. The Rating Community, meanwhile, serves as the discerning evaluators of entrepreneurial creation.

This decentralised community, armed with relevant information and insights, helps determine the worth of enterprises and the potential of investments. Their assessments guide the volume and direction of capital by fostering transparency and informed decision-making. Investors, then, are the consumers of this value. Supported by the Rating Community, they strategically channel their capital towards enterprises and investments, enabling the continued cycle of value creation and consumption.

Each role in this utopian, yet potentially achievable, state is open to everyone, regardless of background or circumstance. Everyone is afforded equal access, creating a vibrant and dynamic ecosystem that encourages participation based on inclination, aptitude, and success. Far from being mutually exclusive, these roles are complementary, promoting a healthier, more inclusive economic system. Recapitalism promises that societal outcomes will improve significantly through systemic measures to broaden access and opportunities. Ideally, everyone will choose to engage in each of the three roles to varying degrees, influenced by their interests and successes in performing these roles throughout their careers.

The result?

An economically dynamic and socially enriched global society underpinned by democratic participation, equal opportunity, and the collective pursuit of unlocking applied creative value. Recapitalism aims to fundamentally redefine how people perceive and interact with the economic landscape. It endeavours to create a vibrant, inclusive, and dynamic marketplace where access to opportunities, financial growth, and the realisation of human potential are more evenly distributed. The path to this destination is navigated through several guiding principles:

Enhancing Efficiency
Recapitalism strives to augment time and price efficiency in the marketplace, promising greater choice and

facilitating straightforward decision-making. It is about forging a synergy between personal and collective interests, igniting innovation and inviting the global population to participate in finance and investing. The goal is to create a genuinely level playing field by optimising the intersection of supply and demand. This is achieved by promoting unfettered participation from a diverse range of participants, effectively breaking down barriers to entry and ensuring the system works for all, not just a privileged few.

Aligning Corporate and Entrepreneurial Interests
Recapitalism seeks to reshape the corporate investment thesis to better align with the aspirations of entrepreneurs. It allows companies to project a more holistic profile to society and their employees without compromising their financial obligation to investors. This encourages a more meaningful and sustainable approach to business, where success can be holistically defined in monetary terms and by the positive impact on society and the well-being of employees.

Decentralising Finance and Investment
Recapitalism advocates a decentralised approach to finance and investing to democratise capital markets. By making the process faster, more direct, and widely accessible, it broadens the spectrum of choice and customisation available to all. Removing unnecessary intermediaries streamlines transactions, bringing a broader array of opportunities within the reach of all individuals.

In achieving these outcomes, the overarching goal of Recapitalism is to realise a more authentic sense of human worth for more people. An individual's wealth is not merely a financial metric but a measure of the quality of their human experience that reflects the extent of their positive contributions to their own well-being as well as that of society at large. The traditional profit-centric approach often imposes constraints on the realisation of this broader conception of wealth. Recapitalism offers a powerful corrective to these limitations by shifting the focus towards a revenue-centric paradigm.

In proposing a Universal Crowd Rating mechanism, Recapitalism fosters the formation of a global community where members work collaboratively to help each other make optimal decisions concerning their finances and time, according to their inclinations. Such a system promises a more inclusive, fair, and productive economic landscape underpinned by the principles of reciprocity, cooperation, and shared prosperity.

Envisioning the future, it is anticipated that if Recapitalism gains traction, its early champions will set a welcoming precedent, inviting all to join this transformative journey. The brave pioneers will transcend exclusive financial bastions by promoting a more comprehensive array of choices and creating fair pricing and return opportunities. They will streamline, automate, and decentralise the roles previously undertaken by traditional intermediaries and illuminate every obscure corner related to informed decision-making in capital markets with the beacon of objective analysis in a form and scale never before seen.

As with any novel paradigm, there will be a vanguard—the trailblazers who bravely venture into uncharted territories and inaugurate a fresh approach. If they succeed in demonstrating the tangible benefits of this new financial system, a diverse array of investment opportunities will surely emerge from all corners of the globe. However, if past trends of new movements serve as a reliable guide, the early stages will no doubt be fraught with pitfalls.

Some individuals, carried away by the excitement of novel opportunities, might recklessly dive into these shallow puddles of fledging immaturity, employing new tools without sufficient thought or preparation. This hasty approach could lead them to construct unsustainable propositions with the new financial frameworks, encountering the risks of unchecked actions before the UCR system gains a functional critical mass. Such instances might provoke a collective reconsideration, leading some to advocate for a return to the conventional, centralised financial systems and a misread reassertion of their supposed roles as the guardians of financial stability.

Nevertheless, the journey won't end there. The initial setbacks galvanise the proponents of Recapitalism to regroup, refine their tools, and deliver education and resources to enhance and solidify participation in this financial revolution. The decentralised version of capital markets with a critical mass of participants can offer pricing, product, efficiency, and availability that centralised means cannot achieve as the quantum of decentralised resources, in the supply and demand of participants are overwhelmingly larger. The cultural shift moves ever slowly until mainstream adoption transcends the former approaches, and eventually, students are taught about the old paradigms in history books rather than in contemporary academia.

Liberation from the primacy of the profit-motive, paired with the harnessing of collective wisdom, could unleash a cornucopia of opportunities for everyone to realise their fullest potential, and to lead lives enriched with purpose, success, and fulfilment. Recapitalism seeks to stir the latent potential inherent in the infinite value of humanity.

"Believing we can make it better"

You're The Voice[3]

About the Author

Adam Gallagher s a public school graduate from a small town on the east coast of Australia who stumbled through an undergraduate Economics degree, a Masters in Commerce and Graduate diplomas in Information Systems and Corporate Governance. His academic experiences provided a near and far view of the behaviours of people, companies and economies, which has quietly preoccupied much of his idle thoughts throughout his working life.

Through numerous professional experiences across debt and equity markets with institutions big and small, Adam gained an appreciation of many different industries and business stages. He has spent the latter part of his career to date in the officeholder and executive ranks of various listed technology companies.

While a party to it though never quite convinced of the merit of the conventional approach to corporate ownership, he watched the decentralised era emerge with great interest. A couple of ideas landed on him, and he felt compelled to heed the call from Pope Francis when in the depths of the pandemic the Pope called for the business world to 'reimagine the economy'. Recapitalism is Adam's contribution.

References

1 Kuhn, T. S. (1962). The Structure of Scientific Revolutions. University of Chicago Press.

2 Pascal, B. (1670). Pensées. (W. F. Trotter, Trans.). Penguin Classics.

3 Farnham, J. (1986). You're the Voice. Recorded by John Farnham. Whispering Jack. RCA Records.

Printed in Great Britain
by Amazon